Silk Scarf
Printing $ Dyeing

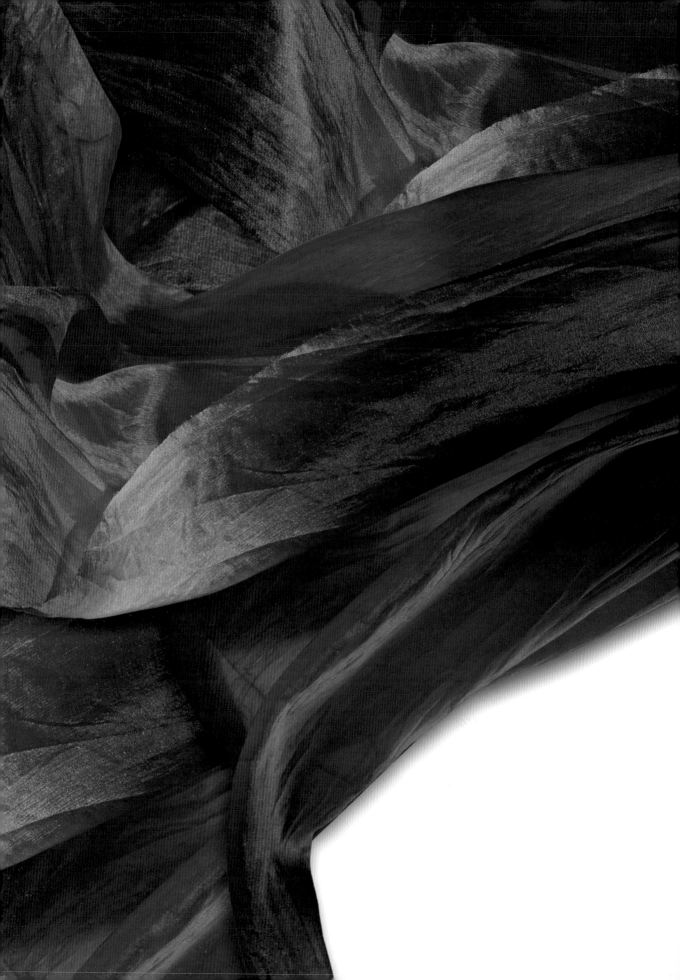

Silk Scarf
Printing & Dyeing

Step-by-Step Techniques for 50 Silk Scarves

Melanie Brummer

STACKPOLE BOOKS

This book is dedicated to my customers who give me daily joy and inspiration. I thank God every day for the amazing work that I have been given to share with such wonderful people.

And to Dad, I wish you were here to see this.

Foreword

Meeting Melanie Brummer at a trade show was quite a frantic experience in a crowd of people during a charity drive. Little did I know that this meeting would become one of the biggest blessings and most joyous events in my life, even if only two words were spoken during that first meeting. She was willing to take me under her wing and mentor me in her craft, as well as the fashion industry where she had worked her way up and gained so much experience. Not only did she become a great mentor, but also a good friend who supports me in everything I do.

After doing some volunteer work and an amazing trip with her as her teaching assistant, I realized that I had discovered a real gem. As a young textile design student with a passion for handmade fabrics, to find a person who shares that passion is very rare. Melanie is just that passionate about fabrics and customizing it by hand. A person who just cannot resist touching a beautiful piece of fabric; seeing it is just not enough. Silk seemed to be her favourite when we met, and admittedly silk is the best and most beautiful canvas to work on.

Melanie had the guts to take her idea and become an entrepreneur. Her mission: to teach her craft and share her vision. Her vision is to establish a culture where people start making their own fabric; which is not only important for the South African textile, craft and fashion industries, but for these industries worldwide.

Her second book is really a great milestone and establishes her as an artist who can juggle between the disciplines of handcrafts and high fashion and is able to bring the two together in harmony. It also fulfils her dream of becoming a serious author and not just a once-off writer.

Helping her work on the samples for the book was a joy. Never in my life had I seen so much silk in one place and it was for us to work on! The deadline was tight and the work was not getting less, but with her guidance, perseverance and encouragement we made it through and created fabulous material for the book. Yet, all the credit for creativity and ingenuity belongs to her as everything in this book was her brainchild.

I believe that this book will give crafters the same joy that Melanie feels when creating an artwork with fabric and that it will teach them that any person can make a fashion accessory that is unique. Melanie describes it as taking a plain piece of white fabric and turning it into anything that you want. It conveys the message that textiles can be handcrafted and customized; that the consumer does not have to be bound to what is sold in stores but is able to create a truly personal style.

The part of Melanie's journey that she shared with me has been enriching and extremely inspiring.
I wish her all the luck in the world and great success on her journey forward.

Clara Jansen
Intern at Slipstream Fabric Finishes cc.

Contents

Introduction

What makes a silk scarf so alluring? Is it the lustre and sheen in the light? Is it the silky feel under your fingertips and against your skin? Is it the fact that it is surprisingly warm in the winter and a fantastic sunscreen in the summer? Is it the fact that the fine silk thread has the tensile strength of steel? Is it because it is lightweight? Is it because it can be rinsed clean and dried in minutes so that you can wear it again when you are travelling? Or, on a more romantic note, because it conjures up images of the Dance Of The Seven Veils?

My relationship with silk scarves goes back to 2004, when I first started dyeing them for the South African fashion Industry. I began wearing them because that is always the best way to promote a new product. It was not very long before I was in love, for all of the reasons listed above, and today I will seldom leave my home without one draped casually around my neck or over my handbag (just in case it gets cooler later in the day).

Today I have a collection of silk scarves in my cupboard to choose from. They are a shifting sea of colour and changing expression. I can tell you that the ones that I have right now are not the ones that I had a couple of years ago. Some of them wear out and literally fall apart from all of the washing and wearing, others get passed on as gifts to loving homes with friends and family, and endlessly I make myself new ones.

I thought I was the only person with this strange addiction, until my students began to confess that some of them were the same. One lady confessed to me that she has 30 different scarves to choose from, one for every day of the month.

This book is for all of you who share my fascination with silk scarves. There are more than 50 different patterns and colourways to choose from so that you can always say that you have the perfect accessory for any event or outfit, and enjoy the thrill of telling people that you have made it yourself when they compliment you on it.

The techniques in this book are simple enough for even a beginner to master. My hope is to show you that you can be more creative than you believe you are currently, that you can make a beautiful thing fairly easily (even on a first attempt) and that the result can be completely wearable.

I hope that by the time you have finished reading this book you are looking at your world with new eyes.

Different ways of embellishing cloth

There are many different ways of embellishing cloth and far too many to cover in this book, which is why I am focussing on simple dyeing and printing only (surface design). I would like to start you off with simple techniques that you can easily master so that you can begin your journey to making your own fabrics with a happy experience.

How do you tell a dyed finish from a printed one?

Before we start, it helps to understand the difference between a dyed finish and a printed one to avoid confusion later in the process. I am always surprised when teaching beginners at how few of them know the difference and it is always worth discussing right at the start. When you look at a fabric for the first time and wonder how it was made, turn it over. If the fabric was dyed, the pattern will be the same on the top and bottom surface of the cloth because the colour saturated through the fibre. If the pattern sits on the upper surface and does not come all the way through to the back of the cloth, it was printed. Fabric paint or ink is sticky and tends to sit on the surface of the cloth.

How do the two processes differ?

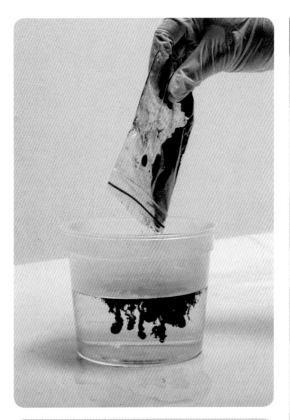

Fabric dye

Completely water-based. Usually the whole garment gets wet in the process.

Wet heat needed in process for colourfastness. This heat can be applied using a gas stove, microwave oven, kettle or any other conventional water heating system.

Auxiliary chemicals needed in process (salt and fixative).

Wet and runny.

Suitable for backgrounds, textures and all-over cover, including tie-dye, shibori, batik and tritik.

Colours blend and mix on the cloth. The colour is translucent (see-through). For this reason a light colour over a very dark colour will have almost no effect.

There is no white dye. White cloth has an absence of colour. If you have a dark cloth that you want white, then you bleach the colour out of it.

For vibrant, dark colours, use less water. For pastel shades, use more water.

Fabric must be washed after the dye has been fixed to remove excess chemicals.

The colour becomes part of the cloth on a molecular level.

The fabric is butter soft to handle after dyeing with a fibre-reactive dye.

These dyed finishes are susceptible to chlorine and peroxide bleaching agents and UV light.

Long shelf life in powder form (years). Liquid mixtures can be re-used with varying results.

Fabric paint or ink

Pigment suspended in an acrylic base. The garment remains dry throughout the process.

Dry heat after the ink has dried for colour fastness. This heat can be applied using an iron, heat press, hairdryer, tumble dryer, heat tunnel or flash cure unit.

No auxiliary chemicals needed. Use ink as it comes out of the container.

Sticky.

Best for graphic pictures and text. Suitable for fabric painting, stamping, lino-block printing and screen-printing.

Colours are generally crisp and differentiated. The colour is often opaque, i.e. a complete block-out that covers the colour behind it.

Because an opaque white paint is readily available on the market, you can print with white ink on any dark-coloured cloth.

For vibrant shades, add more pigment. For pastel shades, add more acrylic base.

No washing needed.

The colour is sealed around the outside of the fibre like a plastic sheath.

The fabric may feel stiffened if you have used ink to cover large areas of the cloth. This will soften mechanically in subsequent washes.

If heat-set properly, these inks are very robust and will usually hold up well under exposure to bleach and UV light.

Approximately 4-6 month shelf life, after which it is prone to mould and bad smells.

Reactive dye

Most reactive dyes are fairly similar. They work in much the same way within similar parameters and conditions. For this book I have worked with my house brand of Slipstream Dye. If you are using a different product, you may want to experiment a little to make sure that it will give you similar results. Different brands package different chemicals from different sources and it is always better to test a sample before you embark on any large projects with a new brand name of dye. Use the instructions provided in the pack for best results. One brand may work differently from the next.

The projects in this book were all made on silks using my house brand of Slipstream Dye, which is a reactive dye for cellulose fibres. If you shop around for other fabrics and work with other brands of dye, I recommend that you run a swatch test first to make sure that your fibre and chemical are suitably matched. Slipstream Dye works best under the following conditions:

- Use the correct kind of fabric with high cellulose content.
- Make sure that the chemicals are present at optimum levels.
- Make sure that they are suspended in water. The chemistry only works in suspension.
- The water must be steaming hot at 65-70 degrees Celsius.
- The colour must be physically battered into the fibre, so expect to work the dye through the fibres if you want the best results. This means that the more you stir the fabric, the more thoroughly the fibre will be coated.
- Give it all some time to work. One hour in the case of silk, 24 hours for cotton fabrics.

Choosing the correct fabric source for the correct dye

Most people are so focussed on the chemicals in the box that they forget that half of the dye chemistry is about using the correct fabric. Dye is fibre-specific. This means that there is a unique chemical for each kind of fibre that you want to dye. As soon as dye and fibre are not ideally matched, results will be variable.

When I was working in fashion, I had a designer who would frequently ask me to dye a fabric that was not compatible with my chemistry. One day I asked him to give me some swatches of these fabrics so that I could show him which ones did not work at all and which ones got variable results, and why. The results are illustrated on the opposite page.

1. The first picture shows how the fabrics looked before we added the dye. This is the "control" so that we have a comparison to work from.
2. This set was dyed with a red, cold water reactive dye. As you can see, the synthetic fabrics did not take up the colour at all and we ended up with the palest pink on only some of the fabrics.
3. This set was dyed with a purple, cold water pigment dye. The most interesting thing about this set is the colour variation between the pieces. Some are bluish and others are pinkish. If you consider that these fabrics were dyed at the same time, under the same conditions, in the same mixture, then this is proof that different fibres will favour different colours in your blends in different ways.
4. This set was dyed with a purple commercial dye that was marked for nylon.
5. This set was dyed with royal blue Rit dye.
6. This set was dyed with navy blue Lanaset. Notice how all of the shiny lycra took the colour beautifully.

1

2

3

4

5

6

Notes about dye colour

You have just seen how fabric source can affect the colour that you get, and just how variable those results can be. You can get anything from very vibrant colour to barely-there pastel.

You have also learned that some fibres will favour some colours in a blend in different ways. So you can dye a fabric in a purple dye that is made from a blend of pink and turquoise and end up with a blue fabric because the fibre favours the blue in the recipe. I have seen this often with silks.

You should also remember that wherever you do not get your process just right, there will be a variance in colour. Red is notorious for this. If your red dye is not hot enough for long enough, it leans towards peach. Blacks might come out navy, grey or brown.

If you want a lighter colour like the softest pastel pink, there are two ways to go about it; you can add smaller quantities of powders, or you can add more water to the powder. It is easy to judge by eye and if you are not sure, dip a piece of white tissue paper into the mixture so that you can see what the colour looks like on a white base. The cellulose in the paper will attract the dye so it is a reliable way of checking the colour.

Notes about dyeing silk

Many books say that you cannot dye a silk with an alkaloid fixative. You run the risk of stripping the sheen off a shiny silk. Unfortunately I only read one of those books after I had successfully dyed thousands of meters of silk this way. I conducted further tests to find out why my information is so vastly different from popular thinking. I discovered that the soda ash does damage some silks after more than 24 hours of exposure. These tests also showed me that silk takes up the dye so easily that you only need to expose it to the mixtures for an hour or so. This seems to be well within the "safety zone" for most silks.

I have dyed thousands of meters of silk using the techniques in this book. If you stick to my instructions carefully, you should achieve the same happy results that I have. I have used numerous different kinds of silk for the samples in this book so that you can see how the different textures, weights and sheens lend themselves to different designs. You will see shiny habotai silk, chiffon, raw silk, crêpe de Chine and even damask. Each one lends its own properties to how the finished work looks and how it drapes.

If you choose to work with cotton, rayon or other cellulose fibres using the techniques in this book, then I recommend that you leave the reactive dye on the fibre for 24 hours before washing for best results.

I usually wash all fabrics before I dye them and bind them up as they emerge from the spinner of my washing machine when they are still damp for best results. While the heavy raw silk might be laundered in this way, the more delicate silks cannot.

Many of them are also impossible to work with when they are very damp. Some of them stick together like a slimy skin when they are wet. I will first test the properties of the silk before deciding whether to wash them and bind them damp or whether it is easier to work with them dry. I have specified in each chapter which technique I used for that project and kind of silk.

If you dye a dry fabric, then I recommend that you squeeze and massage the fabric thoroughly to get the colour through all of the layers of cloth. It will not run in there on its own if the fabric is dry and you run the risk of making a white scarf with tiny bits of spindly colour on instead of the lush coloured examples that you see in this book.

Ideal environment for dyeing

Things to think about when choosing a place to work with dye:

- Good ventilation
- Good drainage
- Easy water supply
- Easy to clean
- Surfaces that do not take a stain like concrete, sand, lawn, etc.
- Surfaces that do take a stain from the dye like PVA walls, white grouting, some tiles and other porous surfaces.

The best place to work with dye is outside in a courtyard, under a carport or under shady trees. I like to work with a hosepipe for easy clean-up and filling of pots for mass production. The projects in this book are all so small and quick that there is no reason that you should not tackle them at home in your kitchen armed only with a kettle and a couple of empty yoghurt containers.

Be aware that the powders will fly around in the air and settle everywhere. You may not be aware that it is even there until there is some moisture in the air and then you will see the coloured spots "rise up" so that you can see them as the dye powder dissolves in the water.

Where you work and what resources you will need will depend on your existing infrastructure and your volumes. If you are making one or two silk scarves for fun or for gifts, then the kitchen, hobby room or laundry is perfect (as long as you wipe down the environment properly with a damp cloth when you have finished). If you want to start a business making dyed silk scarves, then you should consider scaling up and working outside or in a courtyard.

Safety first

Get a sensible filtration mask and wear it if you plan to do lots of dyeing. You can use a paper mask if you are only making one or two projects.

Wear old clothes. Occasionally I will get a student who will ask the question "Will this dye stain the clothes that I am wearing as well?" There is a good chance that it will. Wear old clothes so that you can have fun without worrying about what you are wearing. Black clothing made from polyester or other synthetic fibres will not take stains from the dye.

Wear latex or rubber gloves to protect your hands. I wear two pairs. Does it sound like overkill? When the outer glove gets a small hole in it, the dye runs into the glove and gives you a blue finger that you very often only notice when you take the glove off. To avoid this blue finger phenomenon (or ET Finger as I like to call it), wear two pairs of gloves.

Basic equipment for dyeing

- Water
- Buckets, pots, small containers (anything that holds water)
- Old towels for spills
- A heat source like a microwave oven, gas stove, electric stove or kettle
- Stirring implements
- Hosepipe (nice to have for large projects)
- Thermometer (if you plan to do lots of dyeing)
- String and elastic bands

For many of the projects in this book you will need no more than a kettle, a stirring implement and a small yoghurt container to make your scarf.

Simple dye process

The dye process can be simplified into easy steps. The methodology can be manipulated to suit your specific project, while still fulfilling the requirements of the chemistry. I will outline the simplified process below.

The examples in the chapters that follow are all made using this methodology or a variant thereof. The outline is intended as a guideline only. When tackling individual projects, stick to the exact step-by-steps of the particular project and trust that I have still fulfilled the basic requirements of the chemistry, even though I am exploring a slightly different technique.

- Boil water in your kettle and pour the required amount of steaming water into your container.
- Dissolve the dye powder in the hot water and stir out all the lumps.

- Stir in the salt until it is completely dissolved.
- Stir in the fixative (soda ash) until it is completely dissolved.
- Apply the mixture to the cloth as quickly as possible and stir it into the fibre.
- Leave it to stand.
- Rinse thoroughly.

I call this the "All-In" method of working with reactive dye.

For more detailed information about dyeing fabric, look out for my earlier book, *Contemporary Dyecraft*.

Washing your fabric after dyeing

Dyed fabric must be washed thoroughly to remove the excess dye that has not taken on the cloth. Dye powder gets trapped between the fibres of the cloth. If you do not wash it away thoroughly, it will become dislodged during your first few washes and then it is likely to stain your other laundry. Removing this excess dye is a mechanical process. It requires a physical battering to dislodge trapped dye which is then carried away in the water.

I recommend that you remove the worst of the excess dye under cold running water. When the darkest liquids have run off and you are left with pastel run-off, then you can continue rinsing in a bucket or washing machine until no more colour comes off the fabric. Set your washing machine on a long, cold cycle with a little bit of soap for this wash. The "fail safe" method is to wash items individually. You can rinse multiple items in one load in your washing machine, although the more items you add the more risk there is that something might go wrong.

For delicate habotai and chiffon silks I recommend hand washing only.

The worst thing that you can do with a fresh tie-dye is to leave it lying around in a wet, crushed up heap. This is very dangerous as it can create other marks than the ones that you want as the dye transfers between the layers of fabric. The same bindings that create the pattern also protect the pattern and as soon as you remove them the pattern becomes vulnerable to other unwanted marks.

When you start washing the fabric, do not stop until you have finished to be safe. Then lay the fabric flat or hang it on a hanger indoors to dry. If you hang it doubled over your washing line in the sun, there is a chance that the heat of the sun might create a straight line across the work where it was folded over the line. Luckily, silk scarves are light and dry very quickly, making the projects in this book very easy to wash out.

Printing

Ideal environment for printing

All you need is a table and an old blanket and you can print on cloth. Good ventilation is always essential. The inks and paints give off fumes that smell like ammonia and it is better to work in a well-ventilated room. Wear a mask for added protection and precaution.

Basic equipment for printing

- Blanket
- Water
- Buckets for rinsing equipment
- Old towels for spills
- Stirring implements and spatulas
- Spray bottle with water
- Sponge roller and tray
- Rubber roller for lino printing
- A heat source like an iron, hairdryer, tumble dryer or oven

Plan your route

Plan your route. Plan your route. Plan your route. I cannot stress this enough. Plan your route with projects where you need to line up prints carefully. It is much easier to play out your plan with the lino blocks on the cloth before you apply the ink, than to find out that you are confused when you already have paint on your lino and hands. I always set it up first to make sure that everything fits and lines up before I get messy with the ink.

Make sure that all of your tools and equipment are within easy reach, where you are going to need them during the process, before you start.

Printing table set-up

You can set up for printing the same way for all of the projects in this book. Place an old blanket over the surface of a large table. The blanket creates a soft, spongy surface that lends itself to quality prints. If you try to stamp on a rigid surface, very often much of the stamping surface will not touch the fabric and the ink will not transfer onto the cloth. With the blanket under the fabric, you can push down onto the stamp so that the whole printing surface touches the cloth with enough pressure to transfer the ink evenly. The blanket is the key to clear prints. You might want to use pins or clips to hold your fabric in place. If you plan to do lots of printing, you might even consider using tacky adhesive to hold your cloth in place for printing. When the fabric shifts, it can be tricky to realign it exactly the way it was and if you are printing an image with a straight edge in a tiled fashion, this can cause challenges. The ideal situation is to have a table large enough to lay your entire project out on. Having said this, I have printed very successfully on a very small table with a little bit of patience.

Inking up

The goal is to get an even, thin coating of fabric paint onto the printing surface. Blobs of ink will often result in messy prints. Place a small amount of the fabric paint onto your ink tray. Run the sponge roller through it. Allow the wheel to turn lightly under its own weight. Do not put pressure on the wheel or press down on your sponge. A light touch is all that is needed. Work the ink repeatedly with the roller until there is a smooth skin of ink on the surface of the tray and all around the sponge of your roller. Use the same light-handed technique to roller the paint onto the printing surface or lino block. Ink up from all directions to ensure an even coating of ink on all of the raised printing surfaces.

Transferring the print

For crisp, clear prints it is essential that the ink is pressed into the surface of the fabric. Use a rubber roller to apply pressure to the back of the stamp. Apply the same pressure across the entire surface of the stamp or you risk having lighter areas on your image. This will also improve the wash fastness of the project. With found objects that have funny shapes and no smooth surface over which to run a rubber roller, a handpress with the palm of your hand is very often enough.

The first print

The first print always appears different from subsequent prints and it will stick out like a sore thumb from the others that follow. If you are only printing one image, then this does not matter. If you are planning to tile a piece from edge to edge, then I recommend that you run the first print off as a test print on a piece of paper before you start to print your whole cloth to overcome this challenge.

Handy equipment tips

I keep a spray bottle with clean water on hand. If it is hot or windy the ink often dries out on the ink tray while you are working and it always helps to sprinkle a light mist of moisture over it to maintain the right consistency.

When the ink dries out on the tray, it creates solid bits that cause messy prints. I keep clean, old towels on hand. I like to have a dry towel on the floor (you will be surprised at how often you can get ink on the underside of your shoe) and a couple of small wet towels on hand for wiping ink off fingertips while I am working. Some people also like to keep a small paint brush on hand for touch-ups.

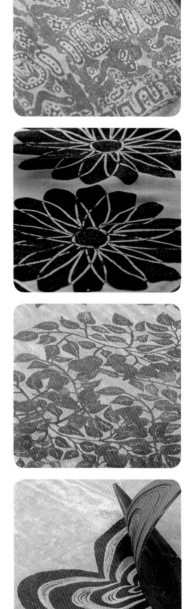

Sponge rollers must go straight into water when you have finished with them. If you leave the ink on them to dry out, it solidifies into a plastic mass that is just not the same to work with. Care for your sponges, wash them out thoroughly as soon as you are done with them, and they will last you a long time. Hook them over the edge of a bucket to dry so that the sponge dries out in its natural rounded shape or you may end up with a flat-sided sponge that is awkward to work with.

Drying time and heat setting

Lino printing and stamping deposit such a thin layer of ink onto your fabric that it air-dries in minutes. As soon as it is dry to the touch, you can heat set it with an iron to the manufacturer's specifications, which is usually something like ironing for six minutes at 140 degrees Celsius.

If your silk will not take the heat needed to set the ink, then set your iron on the maximum setting that the fabric will take and double up your ironing time.

If you do not enjoy ironing or if the project is very large, you can put it in your tumble dryer instead. Any dry heat will work including an iron, a tumble dryer, a hairdryer or even the oven. Although you must remain vigilant at all times with an oven as I have set my fabric on fire before because I forgot about it!

How to make your own lino blocks

Sourcing a good material to make your stamp out of is the first step. Where do you begin?

A LITTLE BIT OF HISTORY

The process is called "lino-block printing" because in the 1960s and 1970s they used linoleum floor tiles to make their handcarved stamps. It was soft enough to carve with regular wood-carving tools. When linoleum went out of fashion as flooring, the quality changed as the demand shrank and the linoleum that you buy in art shops today is a fraction of the thickness of the linoleum that was available during that time.

I am very blessed to be friends with Justine Leroy, who is the grand-daughter of Penny Leroy, who manufactured and exported high-end fashion garments that were embellished with lino-block prints. She was kind enough to allow me to see some of the family's collection of her old blocks and I was fascinated to see how thick the material was in those days.

Essentially it was a linseed oil that was dried out and pressed onto a hessian base to hold it together. Because it was an oil-based stamp, you had to use oil-based inks that took days to dry. The blocks would become brittle and would need a wood-block backing to hold them together. The lino that you find in art shops today is a thin sliver of this material. It can be gritty to carve and is much easier to work with if it is slightly warm.

THE MODERN SOLUTION

Luckily we have a modern solution that I love. While I still refer to the process as "lino-block printing" because that is the terminology that people associate with the basic process, the material that I favour is actually made of rubber. You can now find a rubber mat at art shops that can be carved using wood-carving tools. It is soft and easy to carve and it gives you smooth, sharp cuts. It is soft and pliable which means that you can print in awkward places and across seams. It is easy to clean and robust over time. You can use water-based inks on it. It does not need to be mounted on a wood block to hold it together.

PLANNING YOUR DESIGN

Before you can even begin to plan your design, I recommend that you first learn to "see" the positive and negative spaces contained in your planned image. A simple heart outline can be interpreted in many different ways as this photograph illustrates. Be clear in your mind what you want to carve away and what you want to keep before you start.

This collage of lino blocks opposite shows different interpretations of a simple heart- shaped line drawing. These are all viable ways of cutting out the same pattern, depending on how you would like the end product to look.

Decide if your stamp is going to be a stand-alone image or if you would like to tile it to create other patterns in the repetition.

GETTING YOUR DESIGN ONTO THE BLOCK

If you are confident at freehand drawing, you can draw directly onto the rubber with a pen or permanent marker. If you prefer to trace your design on, then old-fashioned carbon paper is still the easiest.

I also discovered a handy trick quite by accident. I had a pile of flyers stacked in a box under my rubber lino mats. When I peeled them apart a few days later, the ink from the photocopier/printer had transferred onto the rubber mat and I realised that if I just put the photocopied image under the rubber mat with a weight on top for a couple of days, the image transfers itself. Just remember that a stamp will print a mirror image. This means that if you want to carve out text, you must carve it backwards so that it prints the right way around.

Flip your artwork backwards on your computer before printing it out if it is important that it faces in a particular direction.

WOOD-CARVING TOOLS

All you need is a basic set of wood-carving tools to get going. You get two different styles of wood carving tools. One has a blade fixed to a handle, usually with six different shapes of blade on six different handles. The second style of tool is a shaped wooden handle that nestles in the palm of your hand with interchangeable blades.

There are usually three different shapes of blade in different sizes. V-shaped blades make deep, sharp cuts. U-shaped blades scoop out broad, shallow areas. Straight blades are used for finishing and cleaning. Bigger blades are useful for cleaning out large areas, while small blades are useful for detail.

V-shaped Blades

U-shaped Blades

Straight Blades

There is no right or wrong blade to work with. I recommend that you try all of them in every way possible and then decide which one you favour. I tend to enjoy fussing with a small V-shaped blade. A friend of mine cuts bold swathes with the large U-shaped blades and the stamps that emerge from both processes are equally valuable.

If you have never worked with the tools before, then I suggest that you first practise your tool control before even trying to carve on a line. Take a piece of lino and experiment with the different blades in every way that you can think of so that your hands can become comfortable in the process.

Be careful at all times to keep your supporting hand behind the carving edge of the blade so that you do not cut yourself with the tool. Embed this habit when you first start carving and you will spare yourself many small festering cuts. I took a long time to learn this and would frequently go from lino making to dyeing fabric. The salt in the dye would sting and burn and the moisture would cause the wound to fester.

Embed good habits right at the start and you can work freely with the medium.

HOW DEEP SHOULD YOU CARVE YOUR IMAGE?

Once again I encourage you to experiment. Do not take my word for it, find out for yourself and be sure. Practise all depths of cut when you first get to know your tools and then stamp with your practice piece to answer your own questions. Very fine, shallow cuts will print better than you might expect.

Very deep cuts could go right through your rubber mat. This does not matter unless you compromise the stability of the block. This can still be remedied by sandwiching a second piece of rubber onto the back of your carved block.

I will also sandwich two or three layers of rubber together with superglue to add weight to a block that I use often so that a handpress will suffice instead of using a rubber roller on the back of the stamp to save time.

I have sandwiched the block that I use to print my business cards in this way and I have used it to print thousands of business cards over the years. Remember that a stamp creates a mirror image and if you want text, you will have to carve it in reverse.

Although the rubber is fairly expensive, the cost amortises every use and a stamp like this is worth its weight in gold as a daily workhorse.

Different elements of textile design

When I first thought about textile design and breaking it down into logical parts, I realised that it is all very simple actually. Essentially there are only three ways of thinking about designs on cloth. Before you start, you need to decide if it is a Focal Point, a Border or an All-Over Print.

Most fabrics are one, or a combination of these basic elements.

FOCAL POINT
Focal points draw the eye and create a dramatic statement.

BORDER
A border runs along the edge of the fabric.

ALL-OVER PRINT
All-over prints can be scattered organically at random, or they can be neatly tiled edge-to-edge.

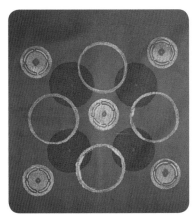
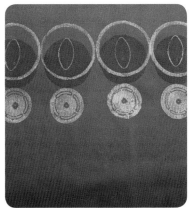
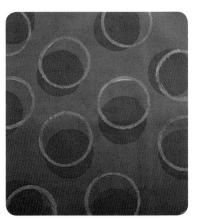

TILED PATTERNS
Tiled prints are a favourite of mine. When I was a child we had some of those garish bathroom tiles with ornate curling patterns on. I often sat in the bath and fascinated over the different patterns that were created by the repetition in the corners.

I enjoy planning and engineering square blocks that, when printed in a tiled fashion edge-to-edge, create other patterns that blur the outlines of the actual block so that you have to take a closer look to find it.

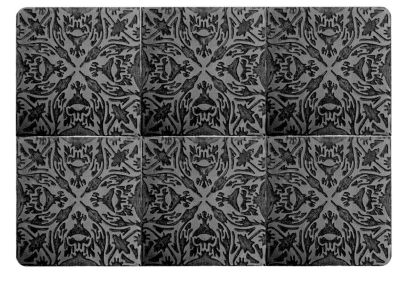

PLANNING YOUR COLOURS
My best advice for planning colours is to try everything.

Sample everything. Appealing colour does not live in the logical side of the brain; it lives in the gut, the eye and the heart. Get out of your own way and stop thinking too hard about colour choice.

Try something new and surprise yourself.

Different ways of finishing silk scarves (hems and detailing)

Half the fun is in the finishing and styling. Essentially a scarf is just a rectangular piece of cloth until you finish it, style it and drape it. You can finish the cloth in a number of ways.

UNHEMMED (DECONSTRUCTION)

The purists cry out at this point. I have dozens of chiffon silk scarves that are unhemmed. The fabric does not run and it is so lightweight, it almost seems pointless. Very few people even notice anything beyond how gorgeous they are when I wear them.

Also, there is a trend in the fashion industry that they call "Deconstruction". A scarf without a hem can be considered to be deconstructed and if styled and worn carefully, you can easily get away with it. I would not recommend this for a fabric that frays easily.

FOLDOVER HEM

Because a scarf is worn draped over the shoulders, the foldover hem may be visible when you wear your scarf.

Make sure that it is neatly done if you go this route. You can turn it into a feature by stitching on a row of beads.

HANDROLLED HEM

A handrolled hem is by far the most discreet way of finishing a silk scarf. If you are lucky, you can find ready-made scarves in white with a handrolled hem.

It can be very tricky if you do not have good fine motor control or if your eyesight is bad.

THE OVERLOCKED HEM

The modern overlocking machine will quickly and easily hem your silk scarf. Just make sure that you use the right needle for the job. If you use an ordinary needle you can very easily punch holes in the cloth and cause snags and pulls.

DETAILING AND EMBELLISHMENTS

The scarves can be embellished further using embroidery, embellishments, sequins, beads and findings. I get excited at all of the possibilities that are available in any haberdashery or bead shop. Use similar colours for subtlety or contrasting colours to make a statement.

Many haberdasheries now carry handmade embellishments that can easily be added afterwards to finish the scarves in interesting ways. They are made from felt, crochet work or sequins. Use felt and crochet work for daywear and sequins embellishments to make a bling statement at night.

Dress your scarf up or down as you need to.

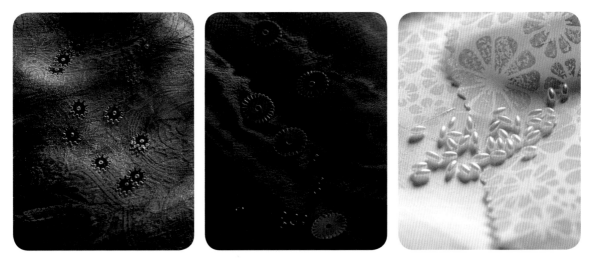

If your embellishments are attached with a pin, you can swap them around as you need to, making the mix-and-match options endless. You can add some bling with useful fittings that you can find at most good bead shops. They have silver clasps that add weight and help the scarf to drape nicely and you can get other interesting connectors and fasteners that you can add for wonderful personal effects.

Interesting rings come in handy when you want to style an old scarf in a new way. I simply pull the ends of the scarf through the ring as a fastener. Large, colourful rings make a striking statement and they are easy to find in matching colours to complement your scarves.

Strings of colourful beads can also be used to great effect. Wear them draped amongst the layers of silk, or wrap them around the silk as a loose fastener.

The styling possibilities for your silk scarves are endless once you begin to explore the options with confidence.

Cleaning your equipment between colours

There are two approaches to cleaning your equipment between colours. The approach you choose depends on what you want to see. If you want crisp, clear prints in one flat smooth colour, then it is best to wash your sponge roller, tray and lino stamp and start working with the next colour with clean equipment.

However, I have learnt that while the eye yearns for a pattern to follow, it also revels in depth and texture. Using mixed colours on a block can produce very pleasing visual effects. I often change from one colour to the next without cleaning the equipment in-between. I simply switch to the new colour and allow it to fade into the work. I favour this technique because it saves ink and water. If you decide to clean your blocks between colours, follow these guidelines:

- After printing, drop the lino stamp directly into clean water and scrub it clean with a soft brush. Dry it properly and store it flat.
- After printing with a found object (plastic and glass), drop it directly into clean water and scrub it clean with a soft brush. Allow to air-dry or wipe it off with a towel.
- After printing with a cardboard found object, leave it to air-dry the ink before you use it again. The milk carton does not wash very well and might turn into papier mâché if you try to wash it. The ink that dries on the cardboard has little effect on the next batch of prints.
- Use the sponge roller to clean all the excess ink off the paint tray and recycle it back into a bottle. Use a butter knife to scrape the ink out of the sponge roller and back into a bottle. Retrieve as much ink as you can before giving the sponge roller a final rinse in clean water. Dry the sponge roller with the sponge side up so that it does not become distorted as it dries.

Caring for your lino stamps

Dry them with a towel and then leave them out to air dry completely before packing them away. Make sure that you store them flat in a cool, dark place. If you leave them in the sun on an uneven surface they will warp, which will make them more tricky to use.

Recycled prints

When I first discovered this craft, my world exploded with the infinite possibilities. Once you begin to "see" the world in this way, you can never go back. It will change your life forever.

General tips for the best prints

Any "found object" with raised surfaces can be used for printing.

You can use an object as it is (in the way that I have for the projects in this book) or you can go one step further and build your stamps from garbage and glue. Cardboard, corrugated packaging and plastic food packaging make fantastic raw materials for creating prints. The soles of shoes and most rubber-moulded products are wonderful for printing with.

Look for items that have an easy grip if you plan to do lots of printing with it.

Apply a thin, smooth coating of fabric paint to the printing surface.

Make sure that you have a way of applying enough pressure to the object to properly transfer the ink onto the surface of the cloth.

Iron the fabric before printing. Creases in the fabric will show in the print.

Remember that the eye is more forgiving than the mind. Do not overanalyse your prints. Stand back and look at them through squinted eyes or take a photograph of the work and look at that before you decide that the work is a mess beyond saving that you wish to abandon.

If you make a "mistake" or mess ink on your fabric, think of a way to make the error a part of the pattern instead, before you think of abandoning the project completely.

Allow your creative work to "become what it is" rather than trying to force it into your preconceived mould (especially if it is just not going there for you). Rather finish the work than end up with a pile of UFOs (UnFinished Objects).

A finished piece can always be given away as a gift if you yourself cannot bear to wear it. Somebody else will likely appreciate it more than you do. Try wearing it before you give it away. You might be surprised at the response you get. Great prints are more about letting go than holding on.

Classic chic checks

QUICK AND EASY

YOU WILL NEED

A plastic block from a child's toy box

Sponge roller and tray

Blanket

Spray bottle with water

Heavyweight habotai silk scarf

Fabric paint in dark green, black and gold

A bucket of water for clean-up afterwards

Iron for heat setting the fabric paint

We are going to create a border along both edges of a scarf for this project. This means that the process below must be applied to both ends of the silk.

1. Use the sponge roller to apply a thin, even coating of dark green fabric paint across the surface of the block.
2. Press the inked surface onto the corner of the silk scarf. Press down on the block so that the ink transfers properly into the surface of the silk.
3. Peel the block away and apply more ink with the sponge roller.
4. Repeat the process along the hem of the scarf.
5. Create multiple rows of blocks, stacked directly on top of each other, using the same technique throughout.
6. Once you have five rows, you can change over to the black ink.
7. Print a row of black squares along the top edge of the green ones. Overlap the green ink with the black ink and turn the block on the diagonal to create points.
8. Once you have completed the black row of prints, you can change over to the gold fabric paint.
9. Insert a row of gold prints along the edge of the black prints.
10. When the ink has air-dried, heat set it using an iron to the maximum tolerance of the silk.

Sports car flash

YOU WILL NEED

A plastic block from a child's toy box

Sponge roller and tray

Blanket

Spray bottle with water

Heavyweight habotai silk scarf

Fabric paint in pink and black

A bucket of water for clean-up afterwards

Iron for heat setting the fabric paint

When I look at this cheeky scarf I can see a lady in large dark glasses behind the wheel of a little sports car with this scarf trailing behind her in the wind as she drives down the highway with the top down.

1. Use the sponge roller to apply a thin, even coating of pink fabric paint across the surface of the block.
2. Turn the block on the diagonal and print it along the edge of the fabric with the points of the blocks along the hem of the scarf.
3. Insert the second row into the spaces created by the first row of blocks.
4. Cover the whole surface of the scarf with pink blocks tiled edge-to-edge.
5. Once you have covered the fabric, you can clean the block in water, dry it off and change over to the black ink.
6. Print black blocks at random angles and spacing over the pink tile.
7. When the ink has air-dried, heat set it using an iron to the maximum tolerance of the silk.

Mondrian inspired me

YOU WILL NEED

A plastic block from a child's toybox

Sponge roller and tray

Blanket

Spray bottle with water

Square raw silk scarf

Fabric paint in black, yellow, red and blue

A bucket of water for clean-up afterwards

Iron for heat setting the fabric paint

This piece was inspired by the work of the famous artist Mondrian.

1. Use the sponge roller to apply a thin, even coating of black fabric paint across the surface of the block.
2. Press the inked surface onto the corner of the silk scarf. Press down on the block so that the ink transfers properly into the surface of the silk.
3. Peel the block away and apply more ink with the sponge roller.
4. Repeat the process to cover the fabric in a tiled fashion. Every few blocks or so you can leave a blank space at random intervals. We will drop the other colours into those spaces afterwards.
5. Once the fabric is covered with the black framework, you can wash everything and change over to the yellow ink.
6. Drop a yellow block into one third of the blank spaces.
7. Wash up and change over to the red ink.
8. Drop a red block into half of the remaining space.
9. Wash up and change over to the blue paint.
10. Drop a blue block into the remaining spaces.
11. When the ink has air-dried, heat set it using an iron to the maximum tolerance of the silk.

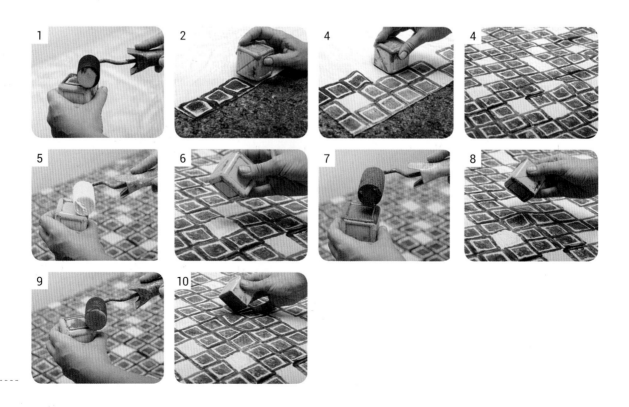

I love to find ways to use really everyday items for printing. The more everyday the item, the more fascinating the transformation becomes for me. The milk carton is one of my favourites for creating tiled effects.

Simple border

QUICK AND EASY

YOU WILL NEED

Two empty milk cartons in different sizes

Sponge roller and tray

Blanket

Spray bottle with water

Ornate damask silk

Fabric paint in grey and dusty pink

A bucket of water for clean-up afterwards

Iron for heat setting the fabric paint

We are going to create a border along both edges of a scarf for this project. This means that the process below must be applied to both ends of the silk. We used an ornate damask silk for this project. A simple border is all you need on an ornate fabric like this one. The simple print is in sharp contrast with the ornate weave of the fabric. I enjoy playing off incongruous elements like this in my design.

1. Use the sponge roller to apply a thin, even coating of grey fabric paint across the surface of the base of the larger milk carton.
2. Decide where you want the border to be placed and create a line of tiled prints across the fabric.
3. Create a second row of prints above the first row.
4. Change over to the dusty pink paint and the smaller milk carton.
5. Drop a row of pink prints into the centre of the grey row.
6. When the ink has air-dried, heat set it using an iron to the maximum tolerance of the silk.

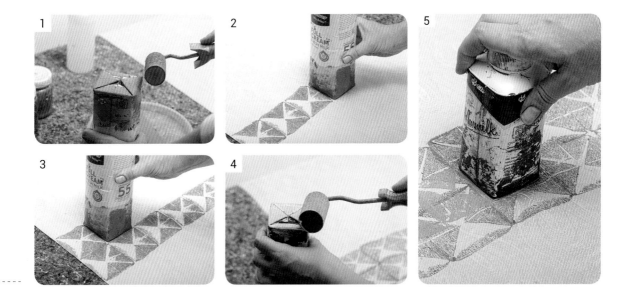

Tanzanian khanga

YOU WILL NEED

An empty milk carton

Sponge roller and tray

Blanket

Spray bottle with water

Satin silk scarf

Turquoise fabric paint

A bucket of water for clean-up afterwards

Iron for heat setting the fabric paint

A simple checked pattern always works well. This print reminds me of some of the textiles that are commonly found in central Africa.

1. Use the sponge roller to apply a thin, even coating of turquoise fabric paint across the surface of the base of the milk carton.
2. Press the inked surface onto the silk scarf. Press down on the box so that the ink transfers properly into the surface of the silk.
3. Peel the block away and apply more ink with the sponge roller.
4. Repeat the process until the whole surface of the fabric is covered (with prints).
5. When the ink has air-dried, heat set it using an iron to the maximum tolerance of the silk.

Layered colour

I love to layer colours and because the colours that we work with are seldom truly opaque, the resulting colours that you get from layered prints can be a complete surprise because the base colour can be seen through the ink of the print. With this project I hope to show you how a dark base cloth can affect the colour of the paint that you are working with.

TO DYE YOU WILL NEED

Habotai silk scarf

Container for mixing dye

Royal Blue Slipstream Dye

Stirring implement

1. Pour just-boiled water into your container from the kettle. Stir in the dye, the salt and the soda ash in the usual way.

2. Stir in the fabric immediately while the mixture is still steaming hot.

3. Submerge it under the surface of the liquid and leave it to stand for an hour before rinsing.

4. When the fabric is dry, iron it before printing, as creases will show in the prints.

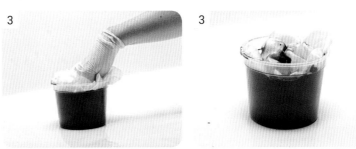

TO PRINT YOU WILL NEED

An empty milk carton

Sponge roller and tray

Blanket

Spray bottle with water

Lightweight habotai silk scarf, pre-dyed in a dark blue.

Fabric paint in red and white

A bucket of water for clean-up afterwards

Iron for heat setting the fabric paint

1. Use the sponge roller to apply a thin, even coating of red fabric paint across the surface of the base of the milk carton.

2. Press the inked surface onto the silk scarf. Press down on the block so that the ink transfers properly into the surface of the silk.

3. Peel the box away and apply more ink with the sponge roller.

4. Repeat the process to cover the surface of the blue fabric with tiled prints using the red paint. As you work you will notice that the colour looks more brown than red as the blue background colour filters through the translucent red ink.

5. Once you have covered the surface of the cloth with the tiled effect, you can change over to the white ink.

6. Print the white prints at evenly spaced intervals over the tiled base cloth. You will notice that the opaque white ink is much clearer on the dark background than what the translucent red paint was.

7. When the ink has air-dried, heat set it using an iron to the maximum tolerance of the silk.

> **Tip**
> Remember when buying ink or paint to check the label on the bottle to see if it is opaque or translucent if you plan to print on dark cloth and still want your colours to be true.

This starburst pattern is a hit wherever I go. It is also very easy to print. The concave shape of the plastic lid from my salad bowl lends itself very well to printing. This familiar kitchen utensil finds a second life in my printing studio.

Barely there

QUICK AND EASY

- A plastic lid from a salad bowl with a pattern that radiates out from the centre
- Sponge roller and tray
- Blanket
- Spray bottle with water
- Heavyweight cream silk with a coarse texture
- White fabric paint
- A bucket of water for clean-up afterwards
- Iron for heat setting the fabric paint

Many people assume that finishes need to be bold or in-your-face to have value. Soft, subtle patterns are awesome and when you print in an ink that almost matches the base cloth you get effects that can be seen at certain angles in the light and that are almost invisible from other angles. Effects like these work very successfully for bridal wear.

I chose a heavyweight silk with a course texture in cream for this project because it drapes so beautifully.

1. Use the sponge roller to apply a thin, even coating of fabric paint across the surface of the plastic lid.
2. Press the inked surface onto the silk scarf. Press down on the centre of the lid so that the ink transfers properly into the surface of the silk.
3. Peel the lid away and apply more ink with the sponge roller.
4. Repeat the process to cover the entire surface of the cloth. Overlap the prints slightly so that you do not have any open blank spaces.
5. When the ink has air-dried, heat set it using an iron to the maximum tolerance of the silk.

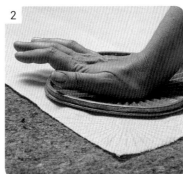

Vintage chiffon

YOU WILL NEED

*A plastic lid from a salad bowl
   with a pattern that radiates out
   from the centre*

Sponge roller and tray

Blanket

Spray bottle with water

Chiffon silk scarf

Fabric paint in gold and white

*A bucket of water for clean-up
   afterwards*

*Iron for heat setting the fabric
   paint*

Create a vintage look with white and gold prints on this gorgeous silk chiffon. Such a finish is ideal for bridal applications.

1. Use the sponge roller to apply a thin, even coating of gold fabric paint to the surface of the lid.

2. Press the inked surface onto the silk scarf. Press down on the lid so that the ink transfers properly into the surface of the silk.

3. Peel the lid away and apply more ink with the sponge roller.

4. Repeat the process and cover the surface of the silk with gold prints from edge to edge.

5. Once the fabric is covered, you can change over to the white ink.

6. Cover the fabric in a layer of white prints from edge to edge. Allow some overlapping of prints and do not overthink the placement. Random shapes will work perfectly.

7. When the ink has air-dried, heat set it using an iron to the maximum tolerance of the silk.

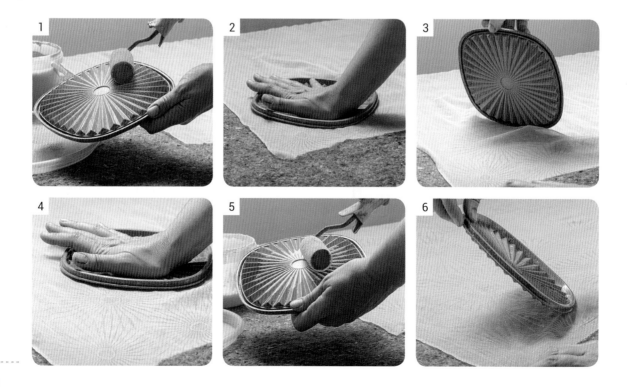

Sunburst sarong

YOU WILL NEED

A plastic lid from a salad bowl with a pattern that radiates out from the centre

Sponge roller and tray

Blanket

Spray bottle with water

Lightweight habotai silk

Dusty pink fabric paint

A bucket of water for clean-up afterwards

Iron for heat setting the fabric paint

Silk scarves also make fabulous beachwear. Print this pattern on a lightweight habotai silk for a summery, translucent feel.

1. Use the sponge roller to apply a thin, even coating of dusty pink fabric paint across the surface of the plastic lid.

2. Press the inked surface onto the silk scarf. Press down on the centre of the lid so that the ink transfers properly into the surface of the silk.

3. Peel the lid away and apply more ink with the sponge roller.

4. Repeat the process to cover the entire surface of the cloth. Overlap the prints slightly so that you do not have any open blank spaces.

5. When the ink has air-dried, heat set it using an iron to the maximum tolerance of the silk.

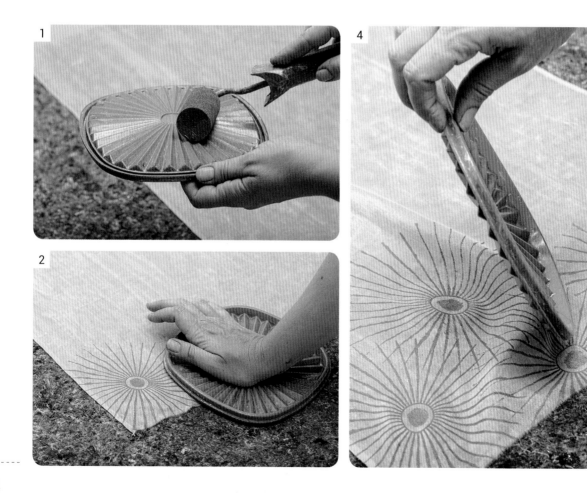

Feng shui urban camouflage

/// **EASY BUT TIME-CONSUMING**

YOU WILL NEED

A Feng shui money-frog

Sponge roller and tray

Blanket

Spray bottle with water

Silk scarf

Fabric paint in camel, rust and teal

A bucket of water for clean-up afterwards

Iron for heat setting the fabric paint

Camouflage fabrics are no longer only used by the military, they have become a staple of our fashion industry. I enjoy looking for ways to make urban camouflage using my own unique colours.

1. Use the sponge roller to apply a thin, even coating of teal fabric paint across the base of the frog

2. Press the inked surface onto the silk scarf and peel it off again. Repeat the process and cover the surface of the fabric with random prints. Space them fairly evenly so that the finished work has an even look.

3. Wash off the frog and ink up the base with the camel-coloured ink. Print the second colour into the spaces between the first colour. Allow the prints to overlap.

4. Wash off the frog and ink up the base with the rust-coloured ink. Print the third colour into the spaces between the first two colours. Allow the prints to overlap at random.

5. When the ink has air-dried, heat set it using an iron to the maximum tolerance of the silk.

Scribbles

Sometimes a very random concept can work really well. This is a fantastic project for those who prefer free play to structured planning.

TO DYE YOU WILL NEED

Habotai silk scarf

Container for mixing dye

Red Slipstream Dye

Stirring implement

1. Pour just-boiled water into your container from the kettle. Stir in the red dye, the salt and the soda ash in the usual way.
2. Stir in the fabric immediately while the mixture is still steaming hot.
3. Submerge it under the surface of the liquid and leave it to stand for an hour before rinsing.
4. When the fabric is dry, iron it smooth before printing.

TO PRINT YOU WILL NEED

A hollow marrow bone with a flat edge

Sponge roller and tray

Blanket

Spray bottle with water

Lightweight habotai silk scarf, pre-dyed in red

Black fabric paint

A bucket of water for clean-up afterwards

Iron for heat setting the fabric paint

1. Use the sponge roller to apply a thin, even coating of black fabric paint across the surface of the base of the bone.
2. Press the inked surface onto the silk scarf. Press down on the bone so that the ink transfers properly into the surface of the silk.
3. Peel the bone away and apply more ink with the sponge roller.
4. Repeat the process to cover the surface of the red fabric with chaotic, overlapping prints.
5. Create a border on both edges of the scarf with the prints.
6. When the ink has air-dried, heat set it using an iron to the maximum tolerance of the silk.

Metallic Africa

A hollow marrow bone with a flat edge

Sponge roller and tray

Blanket

Spray bottle with water

Lightweight habotai silk scarf

Fabric paint in white, gold and bronze.

A bucket of water for clean-up afterwards

Iron for heat setting the fabric paint

This project illustrates the charm of layers of colour. The pattern is scattered randomly across the cloth and there is no fixed formula. Allow the pattern to move and shift as you work. This is a fantastic project for anybody who struggles to line up or register their prints because you can scatter the prints anywhere, in any way, and still get a great result.

1. Use the sponge roller to apply a thin, even coating of fabric paint across the surface of the bone.

2. Press the inked surface of the bone onto the surface of the silk scarf. Press down on the bone so that the ink transfers properly into the surface of the silk. A bit of pressure will help the ink to penetrate the fibre and improve wash fastness.

3. Peel the bone away and apply more ink with the sponge roller.

4. Print the image all over the surface of the fabric from edge to edge.

5. Once the fabric is covered in these random round shapes in white, you can wash the bone in some clean water, dry it properly, and change over to the gold ink.

6. Print the gold shapes in little clusters of between two and six shapes, in a random manner, until you have an even coating of gold shapes across the fabric.

7. Wash and dry the bone and change over to the bronze paint.

8. Repeat the same process that you used for the gold paint with the bronze paint. Squint your eyes and fill in the "empty spaces" that glare at you as you work to create an even look that is pleasing.

9. When the ink has air-dried, heat set it using an iron to the maximum tolerance of the silk.

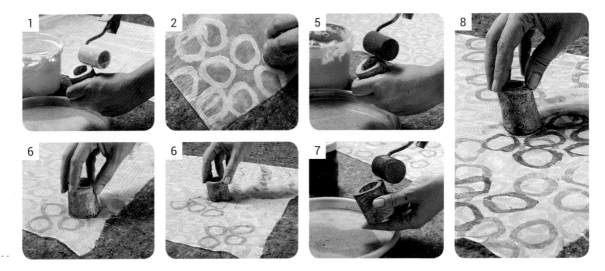

Have a ball

A ball of string can be used in a number of ways to print on cloth. Ink up the ends to make round shapes or roll it on its side for this wonderful V-shaped texture.

Houndstooth

EASY BUT TIME-CONSUMING

YOU WILL NEED

A ball of string

Sponge roller and tray

Blanket

Spray bottle with water

Chiffon silk scarf

Fabric paint in white and grey

A bucket of water for clean-up afterwards

Iron for heat setting the fabric paint

When you squint your eyes at this fabric it looks just like a woven houndstooth fabric. The textured print created by the ball of string gives pointed shapes that suggest the pattern. I decided to play it out in delicate white and soft grey.

1. Use the sponge roller to apply a thin, even coating of white fabric paint across the surface of the ball of string.
2. Roll the inked surface of the ball of string onto the surface of the silk scarf. Press down on the ball of string so that the ink transfers properly into the surface of the silk. A bit of pressure will help the ink to penetrate the fibre and improve wash fastness.
3. Peel it away and apply more ink with the sponge roller.
4. Print the image all over the surface of the fabric from edge to edge.
5. Once the fabric is covered from edge to edge with a layer of white, you can change over to the grey paint and repeat the process. Do not try to wash off the string as you would for a lino stamp. I just roller the new colour over the first one. Because I am using such similar colours, it will not make any difference to the look of the finished work.
6. When the ink has air-dried, heat set it using an iron to the maximum tolerance of the silk.

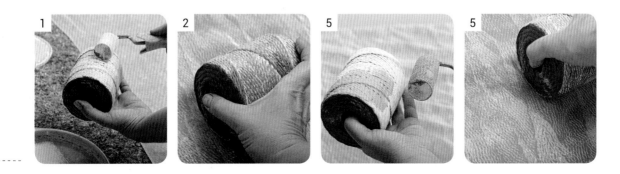

Golden medallions

//   EASY BUT TIME-CONSUMING

TO DYE YOU WILL NEED

Habotai silk scarf

Elastic bands

Container for mixing dye

Orange Slipstream Dye

Stirring implement

This striking project adds an Indian feel to the finished piece. I imagine it will also look very lush on a red or turquoise base cloth. Play around with the same colour paint on different colours of cloth and see how it affects the outcome.

1. Fold the silk scarf in half and line up the selvedge. Fold it again and again in this same way until you have a strip of folded fabric layers about 10 cm wide.
2. Fold that back in half again so that the selvedge from both edges of the fabric is lined up.
3. Scrunch the fabric together and wrap an elastic band very tightly around the end of the fabric, about 2 cm from the edge.
4. Add a second elastic band about 2 cm down from the first one. They must be bound very tightly.
5. Pour just-boiled water from the kettle into your container. Stir in the dye, the salt and the soda ash in the usual way.
6. Stir in the fabric immediately while the mixture is still steaming hot.
7. Submerge it under the surface of the liquid and leave it to stand for an hour before rinsing.
8. When the fabric is dry, iron it smooth before printing.

1

2

3

4

6

7

TO PRINT YOU WILL NEED

A plastic bottle lid with a pattern on it

Sponge roller and tray

Blanket

Spray bottle with water

Lightweight habotai silk scarf, pre-dyed in orange

Gold fabric paint

A bucket of water for clean-up afterwards

Iron for heat setting the fabric paint

1. Use the sponge roller to apply a thin, even coating of gold fabric paint across the surface of the plastic lid.

2. Press the inked surface onto the silk scarf. Press down on the lid so that the ink transfers properly into the surface of the silk.

3. Peel the lid away and apply more ink with the sponge roller.

4. Repeat the process to cover the surface of the orange fabric with randomly placed prints.

5. When the ink has air-dried, heat set it using an iron to the maximum tolerance of the silk.

Recycled prints

Glass bottles

I was delighted to find this glass bottle along the way. The patterned surface makes a wonderful stamp with an Aztec look and feel to it. If you cannot find a square bottle, a round bottle will also work. In that case you will roll the bottle over the fabric instead of pressing straight down.

Aztec silver

YOU WILL NEED

A glass bottle with a pattern on it

Sponge roller and tray

Blanket

Spray bottle with water

Lightweight habotai silk scarf

Turquoise and silver fabric paint

A bucket of water for clean-up afterwards

Iron for heat setting the fabric paint

You can knock together this gorgeous silk scarf in less than an hour and wear it the next time you leave the house. I love the immediacy of these techniques.

1. Use the sponge roller to apply a thin, even coating of turquoise fabric paint across the surface of the glass bottle.
2. Press the inked surface onto the silk scarf. Press down on the bottle so that the ink transfers properly into the surface of the silk.
3. Peel the bottle away and apply more ink with the sponge roller.
4. Repeat the process to create a line of prints along each border of the scarf, about 20 cm from the hem.
5. Wash and dry the bottle and change over to the silver paint.
6. Create a row of prints in silver on either side of the turquoise prints.
7. When the ink has air-dried, heat set it using an iron to the maximum tolerance of the silk.

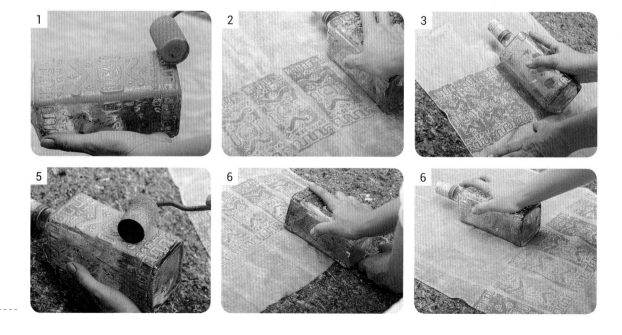

Delft blue

TO DYE YOU WILL NEED

Habotai silk scarf

Container for mixing dye

Royal Blue Slipstream Dye

Stirring implement

Reverse the colours from the previous project, using the same stamp, and the effect is radically different.

1. Pour just-boiled water into your container from the kettle. Stir in the dye, the salt and the soda ash in the usual way.
2. Stir in the fabric immediately while the mixture is still steaming hot.
3. Submerge it under the surface of the liquid and leave it to stand for an hour before rinsing.
4. When the fabric is dry, iron it before printing.

3 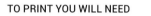 3

1. Use the sponge roller to apply a thin, even coating of white fabric paint across the surface of the glass bottle.
2. Press the inked surface onto the silk scarf. Press down on the bottle so that the ink transfers properly into the surface of the silk.
3. Peel the bottle away and apply more ink with the sponge roller.
4. Print a row of images along the hem of the scarf. Line the prints up edge to edge.
5. Create a second row of prints above the first. Step and repeat the pattern in the spaces between the prints of the first row to build a brick effect.
6. Repeat the process to cover the surface of the dark blue fabric with bricked prints.
7. When the ink has air-dried, heat set it using an iron to the maximum tolerance of the silk.

TO PRINT YOU WILL NEED

A glass bottle with a pattern on it

Sponge roller and tray

Blanket

Spray bottle with water

Lightweight habotai silk scarf, pre-dyed in dark blue

White fabric paint

A bucket of water for clean-up afterwards

Iron for heat setting the fabric paint

Recycled prints

For basket cases

A woven basket makes a fabulous found object for printing. This is another one of those fail-safe prints that seem to work on almost anything in almost any colour. This pattern is very successful for quilting applications.

Vibrating textures

// QUICK AND EASY

YOU WILL NEED

A woven basket

Sponge roller and tray

Blanket

Spray bottle with water

Heavyweight habotai silk scarf

Red fabric paint

A bucket of water for clean-up afterwards

Iron for heat setting the fabric paint

Play around with the same colour paint on different colours of cloth and see how it affects the outcome.

1. Use the sponge roller to apply a thin, even coating of red fabric paint across the surface of the basket.

2. Press the inked surface onto the silk scarf. Press down on the basket so that the ink transfers properly into the surface of the silk.

3. Peel the lid away and apply more ink with the sponge roller.

4. Repeat the process to cover the surface of the fabric with randomly placed prints from edge to edge. Do not be afraid to overlap the prints. The texture created in the overlap is far more appealing than the blank spaces between prints.

5. When the ink has air-dried, heat set it using an iron to the maximum tolerance of the silk.

Lino prints and stamps

Lino prints and hand-carved stamps are a great way of customising your textiles with your own designs. I like to create "families" of prints in different sizes that can be used together in a modular way to create a tight look and feel.

Matched families like these are also wonderful for creating home décor. You can match your napkins, tablecloth and curtains if that is your wish.

The larger stamps are useful for covering large areas of cloth and the smaller ones are ideal for detailing.

General tips for best prints

Apply a thin, smooth coating of fabric paint to the printing surface.

The very first print will usually look different from the prints that follow. If you plan to print multiple images and you do not want this print to stick out like a sore thumb, then I recommend that you run off a test print first before you begin printing on the cloth. A telephone directory is handy for this purpose.

Make sure that you apply enough pressure to the back of the stamp with a rubber roller to transfer the ink onto the surface of the cloth.

Try to keep your fingers and the back of the stamp free from paint for a neater finished product. Work with a damp cloth on hand to use for wiping spills and splashes as you work.

Iron the fabric before printing. Creases in the fabric will show in the print.

Consider the size of the fabric versus the size of your stamp before you start your project. Remember that a smaller stamp will require many imprints to cover the surface of the cloth. If you have a time restraint and a large surface to cover, then opt for larger prints to get the job done more quickly. I have kicked myself on a few occasions when I did not think before I began printing a large piece of cloth with a small stamp.

Remember when buying ink or paint to check the label on the bottle to see if it is opaque or translucent if you plan to print on dark cloth and still want your colours to be true.

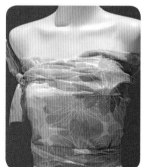

> ### Floral hearts – the Jaclyn
> *My customers loved this lino block I made so much that I turned it into a ready-made stamp. The ornate detail makes for delicate looking prints and I have used it over and over again on cloth, card, book covers, canvas and many other surfaces.*

Layers of love

EASY BUT TIME-CONSUMING

YOU WILL NEED

The Jaclyn stamp

Small floral lino block

Sponge roller and tray

Blanket

Spray bottle with water

Lightweight habotai silk scarf

Fabric paint in pearlescent white and powder blue

A bucket of water for clean-up afterwards

Iron for heat setting the fabric paint

Make this gorgeous project for somebody who is very dear to you (which can also include yourself). We are going to mix it up a little by using a ready-made commercial stamp and a hand-carved lino block on the same project.

1. Use the sponge roller to apply a thin, even coating of pearlescent white fabric paint across the surface of the stamp.

2. Press the inked surface of the stamp onto the surface of the silk scarf. Press down on the stamp so that the ink transfers properly into the surface of the silk. A bit of pressure will help the ink to penetrate the fibre and improve wash fastness.

3. Peel the stamp away carefully and apply more ink with the sponge roller.

4. Print the image all over the surface of the fabric from edge to edge. Overlap the prints to create a continuous film of cover.

5. Once the fabric is completely covered in flowers, change over to the powder blue ink and the small stamp.

6. Print the powder blue hearts spaced randomly on the cloth.

7. Squint your eyes and fill in the "empty spaces" that glare at you as you work to create an even look that is pleasing.

8. When the ink has air-dried, heat set it using an iron to the maximum tolerance of the silk.

Heartfelt blues

YOU WILL NEED

The Jaclyn stamp

Small heart lino block

Sponge roller and tray

Blanket

Spray bottle with water

Lightweight habotai silk scarf

Fabric paint in soft turquoise blue and teal

A bucket of water for clean-up afterwards

Iron for heat setting the fabric paint

For this project we are going to run a line of prints down the centre of the scarf with some highlights in strategic places in a contrasting colour.

1. Find the centre of the scarf and work outwards from there. The hearts will face down from either side of this middle line.
2. Use the sponge roller to apply a thin, even coating of light turquoise fabric paint across the surface of the Jaclyn stamp.
3. Press the inked surface of the stamp onto the surface of the silk scarf. Press down on the stamp so that the ink transfers properly into the surface of the silk. A bit of pressure will help the ink to penetrate the fibre and improve wash fastness.
4. Peel the stamp away carefully and apply more ink with the sponge roller.
5. Print the first two stamps back-to-back starting from the centre of the scarf.
6. Print a row of stamps down the centre of the scarf in line with your first two stamps.
7. Change over to the small heart and the teal ink.
8. Stamp a small teal heart in the spaces between the bigger stamps. The prints can overlap each other. Place three on each end of the scarf.
9. Place one on either side of the bigger hearts on the middle line of the scarf.
10. When the ink has air-dried, heat set it using an iron to the maximum tolerance of the silk.

Scalloped edging

The delicate lacy look of the floral stamp can be used to great effect along the edge of a scarf. We trimmed the raw silk using pinking shears to add to the delicate look and feel. This project shows how effective a subtle colour choice can be.

1. Apply a thin coating of cream fabric paint to the printing surface of the stamp using a sponge roller.
2. Align the first stamp in the centre of the edge of the scarf. Print the image half on and half off the fabric so that just the rounded curves of the heart can be seen.
3. Place a stamp on either side of the first print. This will make the finished work look balanced.
4. Work all around the edge of the scarf in the same way to give the scarf a floral border that spills off the edge of the scalloped cloth.
5. When the ink has air-dried, heat set it using an iron to the maximum tolerance of the silk.

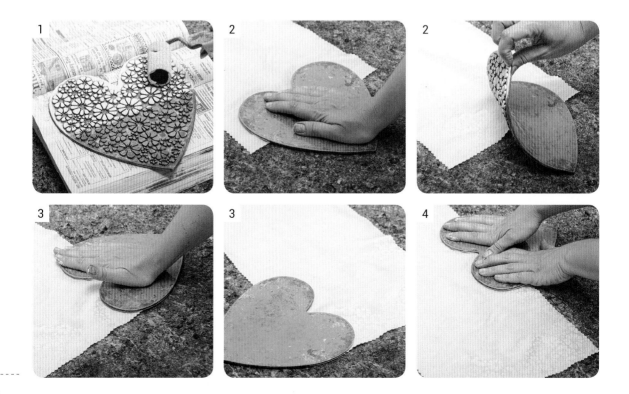

Little black number

QUICK AND EASY

YOU WILL NEED

Small heart lino block

Large heart lino block

Sponge roller and tray

Blanket

Spray bottle with water

Lightweight habotai silk scarf

Black fabric paint

A bucket of water for clean-up afterwards

Iron for heat setting the fabric paint

All that little black number of yours needs to finish it off in a striking way is a silk scarf to match. In one of the previous projects we ran a row of prints down the centre of the scarf to create a symmetrical look. With this scarf we are going to run the prints down the edge to create a more asymmetrical piece.

1. Because the placement of this pattern might be tricky for you at first, I recommend you play it out first by placing the dry stamps in the correct places where you want them to see how they will fit before you begin.

2. Use the sponge roller to apply a thin, even coating of black fabric paint across the surface of the large heart stamp.

3. Place the stamp to the right of the scarf. Press the inked surface of the stamp onto the surface of the silk scarf. Press down on the stamp so that the ink transfers properly into the surface of the silk. A bit of pressure will help the ink to penetrate the fibre and improve wash fastness.

4. Peel the stamp away carefully and apply more ink with the sponge roller.

5. Print a row of stamps down the right-hand side of the scarf.

6. Change over to the small heart.

7. Stamp a small black heart in the spaces between the bigger stamps.

8. When the ink has air-dried, heat set it using an iron to the maximum tolerance of the silk.

2

3

5

Teenage crush

YOU WILL NEED

A large lino heart

A small lino heart

Sponge roller and tray

Blanket

Spray bottle with water

Lightweight habotai silk scarf

Fabric paint in pink and purple

A bucket of water for clean-up afterwards

Iron for heat setting the fabric paint

I used two different styles of hearts in two different sizes to create a border print for this scarf. By using two different colours I was able to add more complexity to the pattern. Young girls love their fashionable accessories and this funky, fresh silk scarf will complement any young teenager's wardrobe.

1. Use the sponge roller to apply a thin, even coating of pink fabric paint across the surface of the large heart.

2. Place the stamp in the centre of the fabric width, approximately 30 cm from the hem.

3. Press the inked surface of the stamp onto the surface of the silk scarf. Press down on the back of the stamp with a rubber roller to properly transfer the ink into the surface of the silk. A bit of pressure will help the ink to penetrate the fibre and improve wash fastness.

4. Peel the stamp away.

5. Change over to the small heart stamp and ink it up.

6. Print a row of smaller hearts above and below the bigger heart, parallel to the hem of the scarf.

7. Wash the large heart and dry it thoroughly. Change over to the purple paint and ink up the large heart again.

8. Print a purple heart on either side of the first pink heart.

9. Ink up the small heart with the purple paint and drop a small heart into the spaces between the small pink hearts. Offset them slightly higher than the first row of prints.

10. When the ink has air-dried, heat set it using an iron to the maximum tolerance of the silk.

Love blues

YOU WILL NEED

A large lino heart

Sponge roller and tray

Blanket

Spray bottle with water

Lightweight habotai silk scarf

Fabric paint in turquoise and royal blue

A bucket of water for clean-up afterwards

Iron for heat setting the fabric paint

This damask silk has a paisley in the weave. There is a heart shape within the paisley that is echoed in the print. To show this delicate detail, I have left spaces between the prints so that the gorgeous damask pattern can show through to complement the pattern of the print.

1. Use the sponge roller to apply a thin, even coating of royal blue fabric paint across the surface of the large heart.
2. Press the inked surface of the stamp onto the surface of the silk scarf. Press down on the back of the stamp with a rubber roller to properly transfer the ink into the surface of the silk. A bit of pressure will help the ink to penetrate the fibre and improve wash fastness.
3. Peel the stamp away and apply more ink with the sponge roller.
4. Scatter the royal blue prints at regular intervals over the surface of the fabric. Leave enough space that there will be white fabric showing between the prints when you have finished.
5. Change over to the turquoise ink and add a layer of turquoise prints in the spaces.
6. When the ink has air-dried, heat set it using an iron to the maximum tolerance of the silk.

Jelly beans (for Clara)

YOU WILL NEED

A large lino heart

A small lino heart

Sponge roller and tray

Blanket

Spray bottle with water

Chiffon silk scarf

Fabric paint in pink, another shade of pink and a peach

A bucket of water for clean-up afterwards

Iron for heat setting the fabric paint

When we were making this sample, my amazing intern, Clara Jansen, said that this piece made her think of jelly beans. So this project is dedicated to Clara and named for her in honour of her contribution to this book.

1. Use the sponge roller to apply a thin, even coating of pink fabric paint across the surface of the large heart.
2. Print the shape randomly across the surface of the fabric. Cover the area evenly so that when you look at it through squinted eyes, there are no glaring blank spaces.
3. Change over to the other pink paint and the smaller heart stamp.
4. Print the smaller heart randomly all over the surface of the fabric. Cross over the blank spaces as well as the printed areas. It is the overlay of inks that makes the end result look so lush.
5. Once you have an even cover of the pink, you can wash the small heart stamp and dry it off.
6. Use the sponge roller to apply the peach ink to the small stamp.
7. Scatter the peach-coloured prints in-between and over the pink ones.
8. Once you can stand back and say "it is finished" you can stop adding layers.
9. When the ink has air-dried, heat set it using an iron to the maximum tolerance of the silk.

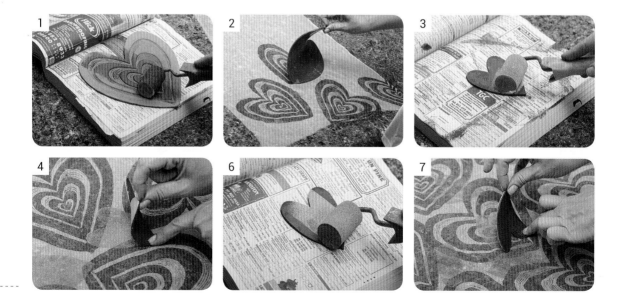

Chic simplicity

YOU WILL NEED

A small lino heart

A small leaf stamp

Sponge roller and tray

Blanket

Spray bottle with water

Lightweight habotai silk scarf

Fabric paint in purple and green

A bucket of water for clean-up afterwards

Iron for heat setting the fabric paint

This is a classic example of "less is more". I always tell my students to keep it simple and one day one of them showed me just how simple it could be with this easy focal point on each end of the scarf.

1. Use the sponge roller to apply a thin, even coating of purple fabric paint across the surface of the small heart.
2. Place the stamp in the centre of the fabric near the end of the scarf.
3. Press the inked surface of the stamp onto the surface of the silk scarf. Press down on the back of the stamp with a rubber roller to properly transfer the ink into the surface of the silk. A bit of pressure will help the ink to penetrate the fibre and improve wash fastness.
4. Peel the stamp away and apply more ink with the sponge roller.
5. Place another in the same position on the other end of the scarf.
6. Change over to the small leaf stamp and ink it up in green.
7. Print a single leaf stamp just below the heart to frame it, on both ends of the cloth.
8. When the ink has air-dried, heat set it using an iron to the maximum tolerance of the silk.

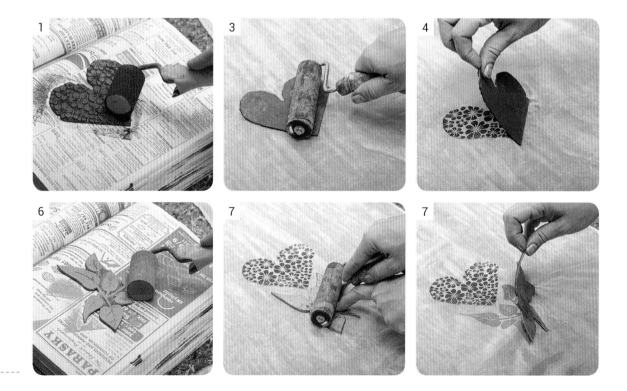

> ## Leaves
> *These leaves have also been one of my most successful concepts over the years. I made this cut-out shaped stamp in three different sizes and they are very versatile because of their organic shape.*

The first shoots of spring

// QUICK AND EASY

YOU WILL NEED

Medium lino leaf stamp

Sponge roller and tray

Blanket

Spray bottle with water

Heavyweight habotai silk scarf

Green fabric paint

A bucket of water for clean-up afterwards

Iron for heat setting the fabric paint

When I was a child there was a huge old oak tree outside my bedroom window. The green of this piece reminds me of the colour of the first flush of leaves that would cover that tree every spring.

1. Use the sponge roller to apply a thin, even coating of green fabric paint across the surface of the stamp. Ink up the stamp from every direction.

2. Press the inked surface onto the silk scarf. Press down on the back of the stamp with a rubber roller so that the ink transfers properly into the surface of the silk.

3. Peel the lino away and apply more ink with the sponge roller.

4. Repeat the process to cover the surface of the fabric with randomly placed prints from edge to edge. Do not overlap the prints. Each print floats in its own visual space.

5. When the ink has air-dried, heat set it using an iron to the maximum tolerance of the silk.

Dip-dyed prints

YOU WILL NEED

Large leaf stamp

Medium leaf stamp

Small leaf stamp

Sponge roller and tray

Blanket

Spray bottle with water

Heavyweight habotai silk scarf

Fabric paint in red, orange and gold

A bucket of water for clean-up afterwards

Iron for heat setting the fabric paint

Sometimes we can replicate dyed visual effects using prints. A dip-dye is understood as one colour that bleeds into another colour. By printing chaotic prints in layers of different colours, it is possible to create a visual effect that looks very similar to the dip-dyed effect.

1. Use the sponge roller to apply a thin, even coating of red fabric paint across the surface of the large leaf lino stamp.

2. Press the inked surface onto the silk scarf. Press down on the block so that the ink transfers properly into the surface of the silk.

3. Peel the stamp away and apply more ink with the sponge roller.

4. Repeat the process to cover the surface of the fabric with red prints.

5. Once you have covered the surface of the cloth with the red leaves, you can change over to the medium stamp and the orange ink.

6. Decide where you would like your dip-dyed look to begin and start your orange prints from there.

7. Cover each end of the scarf in orange prints. Place the prints in the visual spaces between the red layer and allow the prints to overlap to create depth and texture.

8. Now change over to the smallest stamp and the gold ink. Most girls love a little bling and the gold ink gives the finished work a lush look. Decide where you want the most layered colour to be on the scarf and place the gold prints in that area.

9. When the ink has air-dried, heat set it using an iron to the maximum tolerance of the silk.

> ## Floral prints
> Floral prints are always popular and you will find them in almost every collection of fabrics around the world. This stylised floral print is very easy and quick to carve. Notice how a simple colour change can create something completely different, even though you might work with the same stamp.

Evening shade

// **QUICK AND EASY**

YOU WILL NEED

Floral stamp

Sponge roller and tray

Blanket

Spray bottle with water

Heavyweight habotai silk scarf (square)

Fabric paint in black and silver

A bucket of water for clean-up afterwards

Iron for heat setting the fabric paint

Black and silver are classic colours for evening accessories and this square scarf in shiny heavyweight silk will keep the chill out, while looking elegant and beautiful.

1. Use the sponge roller to apply a thin, even coating of black fabric paint across the surface of the floral stamp.

2. Press the inked surface onto the silk scarf. Press down on the back of the stamp with a rubber roller so that the ink transfers properly into the surface of the silk.

3. Peel the stamp away and apply more ink with the sponge roller.

4. Repeat the process and scatter floral prints at random over the surface of the cloth. Leave some space between the prints.

5. Once you have covered the surface of the cloth with the black prints, you can wash the stamp and change over to the silver ink.

6. Print a layer of silver prints in the same way.

7. When the ink has air-dried, heat set it using an iron to the maximum tolerance of the silk.

Pastel pretty

YOU WILL NEED

Floral stamp

Sponge roller and tray

Blanket

Spray bottle with water

Lightweight habotai silk scarf

Fabric paint in mint green, soft pink and lilac

A bucket of water for clean-up afterwards

Iron for heat setting the fabric paint

A colour change can make a dramatic difference. While we will use the same print for this scarf as we did in the previous project, the change of colour turns a chic evening accessory into funky daywear.

1. Use the sponge roller to apply a thin, even coating of mint green fabric paint across the surface of the floral stamp.
2. Press the inked surface onto the silk scarf. Press down on the block so that the ink transfers properly into the surface of the silk.
3. Peel the stamp away and apply more ink with the sponge roller.
4. Repeat the process to cover the surface of the fabric with scattered mint green prints.
5. Once you have covered the surface of the cloth with the mint green prints, you can wash the stamp and change over to the soft pink ink.
6. Add a layer of soft pink prints in the spaces between the green ones. Allow the prints to overlap in places.
7. Squint your eyes as you work to see if there are any visual empty spaces that still need to be filled before moving onto the third colour.
8. Wash the stamp and change over to the lilac paint.
9. Drop on a few lilac shapes to add depth and interest.
10. When the ink has air-dried, heat set it using an iron to the maximum tolerance of the silk.

Organic rounds

Round, organic shapes make awesome lino prints. They can easily be pieced together for all-over cover and they are just as effective on their own as focal points. String them together like beads in a row and play with different sizes and colours. I was inspired by a beautiful round shape in a tie-dye. I took a photograph of the shape and then printed it out in three different sizes to create this set of lino blocks.

String of beads

QUICK AND EASY

YOU WILL NEED

A set of organic looking round lino blocks in three different sizes

Sponge roller and tray

Blanket

Telephone directory

Spray bottle with water

Heavyweight habotai silk scarf

Fabric paint in mustard and dark brown.

A bucket of water for clean-up afterwards

Iron for heat setting the fabric paint

Prints along the centre panel of the scarf are very effective. They are equally effective as table runners. If you are looking for a multi-purpose fabric that you can use for both clothing and homeware, then a pattern down the centre panel lends itself to both uses.

1. Mark the centre of the fabric with a pin so that you know exactly where you want to place the first print.
2. Place the lino block on a clean page in a telephone directory. Use the sponge roller to apply a thin, even coating of fabric paint across the surface of the larger of the shapes. Close the book and press down on it with your hand. The pressure that you apply will transfer the paint onto a page of the book and you can see how it is going to look.
3. Place the lino on the silk in the correct position and apply even pressure to the back of the stamp using a rubber roller to make sure that you properly transfer the ink into the surface of the fabric.
4. Repeat the pattern in a straight line in the centre of the cloth. You can print five shapes in total. I placed two on either side of the middle one.
5. Change over to the smaller shape and ink it up.
6. Print the smaller shapes in a line down the centre of the scarf up to each end.
7. Wash the lino stamp that you are working with, dry it off well, and apply the dark brown paint to it.
8. Once you have run your test print, you can print the darker shapes offset into the space between the mustard shapes.

9. Finish off with rounds inset into the spaces on either side of the first five prints.

10. When the ink has air-dried, heat set it using an iron to the maximum tolerance of the silk and wear with pride.

Winter black

TO DYE YOU WILL NEED

Raw silk with a gritty texture

Container for mixing dye

Black Slipstream Dye

Stirring implement

For a scarf that is warmer with a heavier weight and drape, I used a raw, unfinished silk slub with a gritty texture. The heavier fabric lends itself to darker colours and I thought it would be lovely in black and white.

1. Pour just-boiled water into your container from the kettle. Stir in the dye, the salt and the soda ash in the usual way.
2. Stir in the fabric immediately while the mixture is still steaming hot.
3. Submerge it under the surface of the liquid and leave it to stand for an hour before rinsing.
4. When the fabric is dry, iron it before printing.

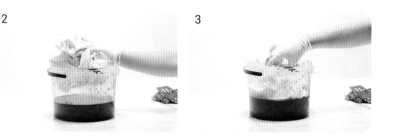

TO PRINT YOU WILL NEED

Medium organic round stamp

Sponge roller and tray

Blanket

Spray bottle with water

Pre-dyed heavyweight raw silk

White fabric paint

A bucket of water for clean-up afterwards

Iron for heat setting the fabric paint

1. Use the sponge roller to apply a thin, even coating of white fabric paint across the surface of the stamp.
2. Press the inked surface onto the silk scarf. Press down on the back of the stamp with a rubber roller so that the ink transfers properly into the surface of the silk.
3. Peel the stamp away and apply more ink with the sponge roller.
4. Cover the fabric from edge to edge with white prints. Because they are round it is easy to place them very close together, although they do not overlap. Some of them spill off the edge of the cloth.
5. When the ink has air-dried, heat set it using an iron to the maximum tolerance of the silk.
6. I found this gorgeous crochet flower on a pin that I use to hold it in place.

> ## African inspiration
>
> *I was inspired by geometric African designs to create this set of lino blocks that can be used to create all-over tiled effects and focal points. The large rectangular stamps are useful for all-over tiled cover, while the shaped cut-outs are wonderful for borders, detailing and focal points.*

Icon

// **EASY BUT TIME-CONSUMING**

TO DYE YOU WILL NEED

Lightweight habotai silk

Container for mixing dye

Dark Green Slipstream Dye

Stirring implement

I made this small cut-out stamp as a complement to this family of stamps. The shape has always reminded me a little of the battleships in some of the computer games when I was a child.

White ink is successful on almost any background colour. Use it when you are not sure what colour you should use. It is a great default to fall back on if you run out of inspiration. Gold and black are also great default colours to use if you feel afraid about any other colour choice.

This is a good place to start if you are a beginner who wants to try out a little bit of easy dyeing and a little bit of easy printing in one project.

1. Pour just-boiled water into your container from the kettle. Stir in the dye, the salt and the soda ash in the usual way.
2. Stir in the fabric immediately while the mixture is still steaming hot.
3. Submerge it under the surface of the liquid and leave it to stand for an hour before rinsing.
4. When the fabric is dry, iron it before printing.

1. Figure out exactly where you plan to place your stamps before you put ink on it. I placed this row of stamps 15 cm from the edge of the fabric and because there are three shapes, I was able to start in the centre with the first one, and then just place one on either side in a line to finish the design.

2. Use the sponge roller to apply a thin, even coating of white fabric paint across the surface of the stamp.

3. The first print will look different from the prints that follow and this will be unsightly on a piece like this. For this reason I run off a test print onto the telephone book first, before inking up and placing the first print on the cloth.

4. Place the stamp in the position that you planned for it.

5. Press the inked surface onto the silk scarf. Press down on the back of the stamp with a rubber roller so that the ink transfers properly into the surface of the silk.

6. Peel the stamp away and apply more ink with the sponge roller.

7. Place another stamp on either side of the first stamp.

8. Then place a final shape above the first stamp.

9. When the ink has air-dried, heat set it using an iron to the maximum tolerance of the silk.

Nautical geometry

YOU WILL NEED

Rectangular geometric lino block

Shaped geometric lino block

Sponge roller and tray

Blanket

Spray bottle with water

Lightweight habotai silk scarf in white

Nautical blue and red fabric paint

A bucket of water for clean-up afterwards

Iron for heat setting the fabric paint

A colour change can make a similar concept look quite different by the time it is finished. This scarf has a nautical look and feel because of the colouring. In this example we will add a layer of detail over the tiled base coat using a cut-out shape. Notice how I used a part of the motif from the bigger stamp to create the pattern for the cut-out so that the two pieces will always work together as a matched pair.

1. Use the sponge roller to apply a thin, even coating of nautical blue fabric paint across the surface of the stamp.

2. Position the first print along the hem of the scarf and in the centre. This will leave an equal amount of space on either side of the first print. By centering the pattern with the first print, the whole pattern will appear more balanced to the eye. Press the inked surface onto the silk scarf and apply pressure using a rubber roller so that the ink transfers properly into the surface of the silk.

3. Peel the stamp away carefully and apply more ink with the sponge roller.

> **Tip** The fabric might move when you peel off the stamp and you may need to adjust it so that the edge of the print appears straight again before trying to line up the second print next to a print with a wavy edge. You might prefer to clamp your work down in some way with crocodile clamps, pins or some other mechanism to avoid this.

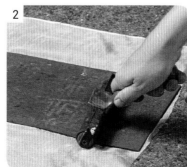

Lino prints and stamps

4. Place the second print to the right of the first print and the third one to the left, using the same technique as for the first one.

5. Line up the second row of prints using the centre print as a guideline.

6. Carry on in this way until you have covered the whole surface of the cloth.

7. When the ink has air-dried, change over to the shaped stamp and the red ink.

8. Place the first red stamp in the centre of the scarf, about 10 cm from the end of the scarf so that you still have space to hem and finish it afterwards.

9. Make sure that you get even pressure on the back of the stamp with a rubber roller so that the ink transfers clearly.

10. Run a row of red prints right down the centre of the scarf, placing them tip to tip, with about 2 cm between them.

11. Once the ink has air-dried, heat set it using an iron to the maximum tolerance of the silk.

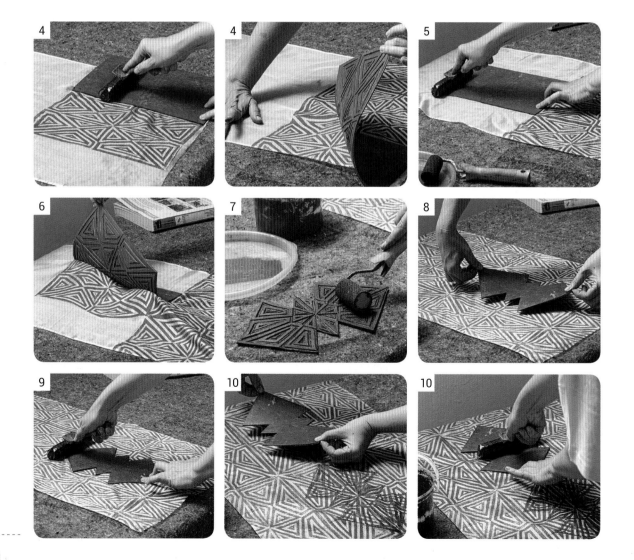

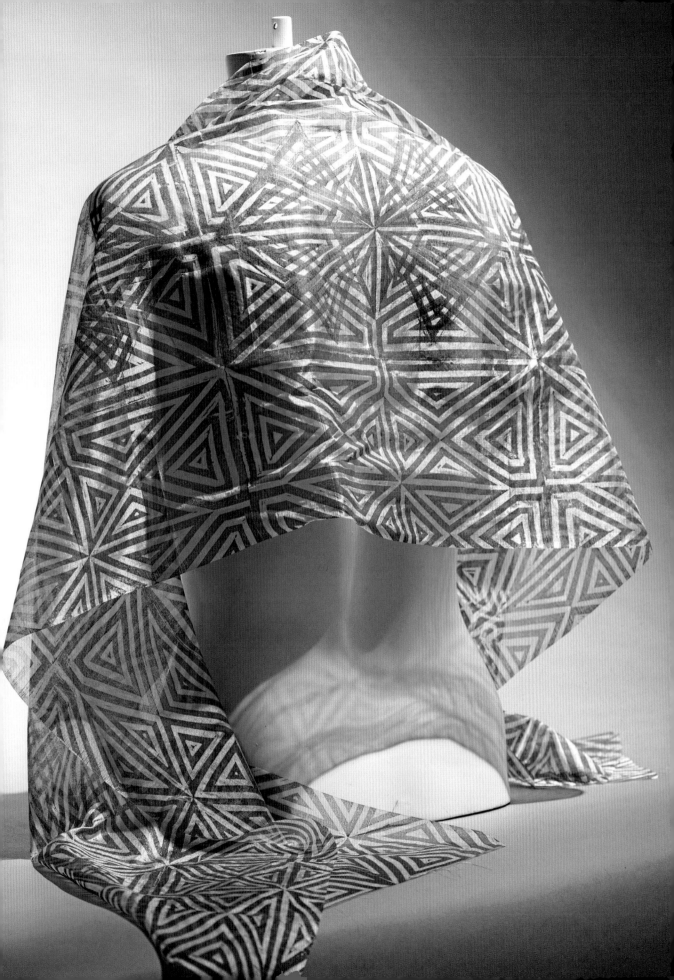

Tie-dyed scarves

When you print a scarf, it develops in front of your eyes as planned. The outcome is fairly predictable and you see the work take shape while you are working. When you dye a scarf, the fabric is submerged under fluid and bound up into alien shapes that are unrecognisable from the patterns that they are actually making; you cannot see what you are doing for much of the process.

It is only at the end, after the bindings have come off and the fabric has been laundered thoroughly and dried, that you finally get to see what you have made. It is a magical part of the process that I call "The Wow Moment!".

While the words may sound clichéd, these are the words that most often spill from human lips when the beautiful patterns finally emerge from their bindings like butterflies.

General tips for best results

Plan your route. Go over the plan again. Go over the plan one final time as you set everything up where you need it. Do a dry run if you are still not clear before actually opening the bags of dye. Once you are sure that you know exactly what you are doing, launch into the project and mix the dye.

This advice is good for beginners and experienced dyers. When I mass-produced for the fashion industry, there would be times when I would have 350 garments to tie-dye that all had to look the same for retail purposes. My tolerance for "variance" was under 5% on most of my production or I would offer to buy the stock from the customer if it was over 10%.

This methodology of careful planning was the only way I could ensure that my business remained sustainable.

Even if you are only making one small project, it is still good advice. Usually if you are only making one, you are quite attached to the outcome, especially if it is a gift or if you plan to wear it yourself that evening to finish off an outfit for an important event.

Because silk is expensive, you might also be attached to the outcome. Save yourself some heartache. Decide before you start how important it is to you to get a good result. Allow this to inform how much planning you will need for these dyed projects.

Most importantly though, have fun!

Corporate chic

YOU WILL NEED

Rectangular silk scarf in heavy-weight habotai

Two elastic bands

Red and Navy Slipstream Dye

Container for mixing dye

Kettle and hot water

Stirring implement

Crocodile clamp

Empty bucket

This stunning silk scarf will finish a navy corporate suit to make a confident statement at any meeting. Choose structured geometric patterns in corporate colours like black, navy and red to accessorise your simple suits.

1. Work with damp fabric.
2. Line up the two ends of the scarf so that the pattern is mirrored on both ends. This will give the finished work a balanced look and make it quicker and easier to bind.
3. Fold the fabric in half along the hems of the scarf.
4. Create more concertina folds along the hems until you end up with a strip of folded fabric about 5 cm wide.
5. Decide where you would like your blue border to begin, place your palm on the fabric at this point and use it to create your first fold at 90 degrees to the first concertina folds.
6. Make concertina folds in the other direction, about 5 cm in width, so that you end up with a little square folded shape with a long, flat tail.

7. Tie a very tight elastic band around the fabric, about 15 cm from the hem edge.

8. Add a second elastic band 2 cm from the first one. They must be very tight.

9. Fill the container with very hot water from the kettle and mix in the red dye, the salt and the soda ash in the usual way. Stir until all of the lumps are dissolved.

10. Place the scarf in the dye up to the place where you want the red to end and attach it to the edge of the container with a crocodile clamp to hold it in place.

11. Leave it to stand for an hour.

12. Remove the scarf from the red dye and squeeze the excess dye out.

13. Mix a small quantity of the navy blue dye in a container. You need just enough to comfortably cover the piece of scarf on the end that you want to make navy.

14. Place the larger bucket next to the container so that you can use the crocodile clamp to hold it in place for an hour.

15. Remove the fabric from the dye, squeeze out the excess dye and wash well in clean water until the water runs clear and no more colour comes out.

16. Add a small dash of fabric softener to the last rinse for softness.

11

14

14

Diagonal checks

/// **MEDIUM DIFFICULTY**

YOU WILL NEED

Square silk scarf

Two elastic bands

Purple Slipstream Dye

Container for mixing dye

Kettle and hot water

Stirring implement

It is possible to create checked patterns with tie-dye. The structure of the fabric will govern how crisp and clear these geometric designs come out. The silk that I used for this project is quite floppy so the pattern is a little distorted. Crisper fabrics will give clearer checks.

1. Work with damp fabric.
2. Fold the fabric on the diagonal from corner to corner.
3. Create concertina folds parallel to that first fold, until you end up with a strip of fabric about 7 cm wide.
4. Fold the strip back in half.
5. Create more concertina folds parallel to the first one until you end up with a square shape about 7 cm across in both directions.
6. Place a loose elastic band around the shape in both directions across the centre line. The idea is to get the placement correct before the fabric becomes distorted by the tightening.
7. By placing them loosely where we need them it is easier to then tighten the elastic bands up in the right place. Make sure that they are very tight so that you can see the checked pattern at the end.
8. Fill the container with very hot water from the kettle and mix in the purple dye, the salt and the soda ash in the usual way. Stir until all of the lumps are dissolved.
9. Place the scarf in the dye, jiggle it around a little and make sure that it is submerged under the liquid.
10. Leave it to stand for an hour.
11. Remove the fabric from the dye, squeeze out the excess dye and wash well in clean water until the water runs clear and no more colour comes out.
12. Add a small dash of fabric softener to the last rinse for softness.

Tie-dyed scarves

Hot pink mosaic

YOU WILL NEED

Rectangular chiffon silk scarf

Two elastic bands

Pink, Golden Yellow and Purple Slipstream Dye

Container for mixing dye

Kettle and hot water

Stirring implement

Crocodile clamp

Although we will be binding the same checked pattern as in the previous project, the chiffon silk that we will be using for this project has even less structural stability than the silk that we used before, so the checked pattern morphs into more of an organic mosaic pattern.

1. Work with damp fabric.
2. Fold the fabric in the length down the selvedge multiple times until you have a strip of folded fabric about 10 cm wide.
3. Fold the strip back in half.
4. Create more concertina folds parallel to this fold until you end up with a square shape about 10 cm across in both directions.
5. Place a loose elastic band around the shape in both directions across the centre line. The idea is to get the placement correct before the fabric becomes distorted by the tightening.
6. By placing them loosely where we need them it is easier to then tighten the elastic bands up in the right place. Make sure that they are very tight so that you can see the checked pattern at the end.
7. Fill the container with very hot water from the kettle and mix in the pink dye, the salt and the soda ash in the usual way. Stir until all of the lumps are dissolved.

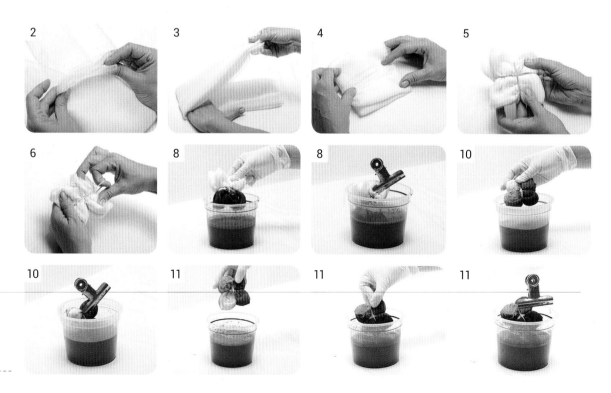

8. Place the scarf in the dye up to the middle line where the elastic band is, and use the crocodile clamp to attach it to the side of the bucket.

9. Leave it to stand for an hour.

10. Remove the fabric from the dye and squeeze out the excess. Mix the golden yellow dye in the usual way, turn the fabric with the pink facing to the right, and submerge it in the yellow dye up to the elastic band. Attach a crocodile clamp to keep it in place.

11. Remove the fabric from the dye and squeeze out the excess dye. Mix the purple dye in the usual way, turn the fabric around, and submerge the section that is still white in the purple dye. Attach a crocodile clamp to keep it in place.

12. Wash this lightweight scarf out under clean running water.

13. Add a small dash of fabric softener to the last rinse for softness.

Stormy electricity

YOU WILL NEED

Crêpe de Chine silk scarf

Four elastic bands

Navy Slipstream Dye

Container for mixing dye

Kettle and hot water

Stirring implement

For this project I used crêpe-de-Chine. This fabric drapes beautifully so I made a larger piece to drape and pin in creative ways. This is the easiest way to create a border on any piece of cloth. The navy colour makes it versatile as daywear and corporate wear. Dress it down with your denims or up with your chic corporate suits.

1. Work with damp fabric.
2. Take the fabric along the cut edge and fold it in half so that the two cut edges line up.
3. Gather the fabric into loose concertina folds along this cut edge.
4. Wrap a very tight elastic band around the fabric in an open position. Add a second one below that in the same way to create a strip of elastic bands about 15 cm wide.
5. Add enough water from your just-boiled kettle to the container to cover the project. Mix in the navy dye, the salt and the soda ash in the usual way. Stir until all of the lumps are dissolved.
6. Place the scarf in the dye, jiggle it around a little and make sure that it is submerged under the liquid.
7. Leave it to stand for an hour.
8. Remove the fabric from the dye, squeeze out the excess dye and wash well in clean water until the water runs clear and no more colour comes out.
9. Add a small dash of fabric softener to the last rinse for softness.

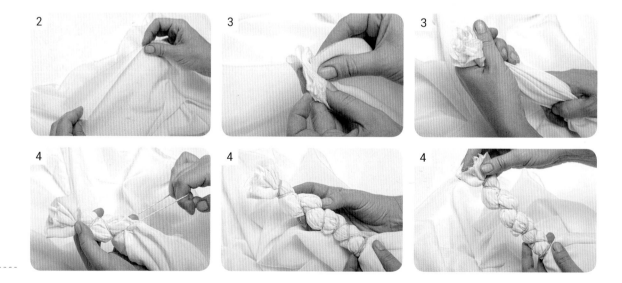

Cobweb charm

YOU WILL NEED

Rectangular lightweight habotai silk scarf

A few elastic bands

Turquoise and Brown Slipstream Dye

Container for mixing dye

Kettle and hot water

Stirring implement

Crocodile clamp

This project is very easy and it always creates a happy result, provided you get your elastic bands tight enough. This fail-safe pattern is a great place to start for beginners who are nervous. I often use this pattern for demonstrations during my classes and it always delights my students with its magical outcome.

1. Work with dry fabric. This silk sticks to itself when it is wet.
2. Find the centre of the scarf, grip the fabric between your fingers at that point, and pull the fabric into a teat.
3. Bind elastic bands very tightly along the length of the fabric to create a long snake of bound-up cloth.
4. Fill the container with very hot water from the kettle and mix in the turquoise dye, the salt and the soda ash in the usual way. Stir until all of the lumps are dissolved.
5. Place the scarf in the dye, jiggle it around a little and make sure that it is submerged under the liquid.
6. Leave it to stand for an hour.
7. Remove the fabric from the dye, squeeze out the excess dye and mix half a container of hot brown dye.
8. Roll the snake up into a coil and submerge half of the coil in the brown dye. Jiggle it a little so that the colour can penetrate the cloth. Attach the scarf to the side of the container using the crocodile clamp to hold it in place.
9. Leave it to stand for an hour.
10. Remove the fabric from the dye, squeeze out the excess dye and wash well in clean water until the water runs clear and no more colour comes out.

2

3

5

6

8

8

110

Fantasy under the sea

YOU WILL NEED

Patience

Chiffon silk scarf

Many elastic bands

Turquoise, Lime Green and Purple Slipstream Dye

Container for mixing dye

Kettle and hot water

Stirring implement

Crocodile clamp

Although this project looks similar to the one before, because you are binding multiple shapes, it will take you longer to tie up the cloth. Do not embark on this project if you are in a hurry. The extra effort is well worth the extra work, though, and I find this pattern captivating.

I have manufactured this finish many times for the fashion industry in many different colour ways and it is a guaranteed success every time. I chose colours from the sea for this one so that I can wear it as a sarong on the beach.

1. Work with dry fabric.
2. Choose a place to begin your first shape. With a pattern like this, it can be anywhere. Do not overthink it. Grip the fabric between your fingers at that point, and pull the fabric into a spike.
3. Bind very tight elastic bands along the length of the fabric to create a spike of bound-up cloth about 10 cm long.
4. Choose another centre about 15 cm from the first shape, pull the fabric taut between the two points and shift that down into another spike shape. Bind this up tightly with another elastic band.
5. Continue in this manner until you have bound up all of the fabric into multiple spikes. The finished item looks a little like a squid.
6. Fill the container with very hot water from the kettle and mix in the turquoise dye, the salt and the soda ash in the usual way. Stir until all of the lumps are dissolved.
7. Place the scarf in the dye, jiggle it around a little and make sure that it is submerged under the liquid.

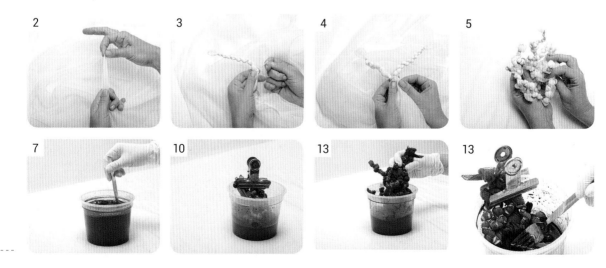

8. Leave it to stand for an hour.

9. Remove the fabric from the dye, squeeze out the excess dye and mix half a container of hot lime green dye.

10. Place half of the fabric into the lime green dye and attach it to the side of the container using the crocodile clamp.

11. Leave it to stand for an hour.

12. Remove the fabric from the dye, squeeze out the excess dye and mix half a container of hot purple dye.

13. Place half of the green and half of the turquoise fabric into the purple and attach the rest to the side of the container using the crocodile clamps, keeping the colours separated.

14. Leave it to stand for an hour.

15. Remove the fabric from the dye, squeeze out the excess dye and wash well in clean water until the water runs clear and no more colour comes out.

16. Add a small dash of fabric softener to the last rinse for softness.

Tie-dyed scarves

Dip-dyeing (or ombre)

YOU WILL NEED

Patience

Damask silk scarf

3 x Brown Slipstream Dye

Two containers for mixing chemicals

Gas bottle or stove

Large pot

Stirring implements

Measuring cup

Spray bottle

Coat hanger

Clothing rail or pole

Ski rope

A brick with holes in

Although many people view dip-dyeing as a form of tie-dyeing, I prefer to think of it more in terms of a smooth, flat colour that you are bleeding on in a very controlled way. I feel this way because we do not use a single elastic band or piece of string to bind the cloth. This technique takes a high level of concentration to get the colour absolutely smooth and splash-free.

It is also very beautiful and trendy in the fashion capitals around the world and if you have the courage to try this technique for yourself, you will be greatly rewarded.

For this project I used a damask silk with a paisley in the weave to add subtle detail to the simple finish. I worked directly onto the creamy background cloth, which works well with the dark brown dye.

1. Start by building a structure that you can hang your fabric from. I used a clothing rail for this project. You might find that a washing line or a pole between two walls might work as well for you, depending on the size of your project and what heat source you decide to use. I hang the fabric over a coat hanger and then suspend that from ropes going over the top of the clothing rail. The brick is attached to the end of the ropes as a counterweight so that the fabric does not slip into the pot of dye completely. This contraption allows me to slowly raise and lower the fabric into the dye as I need to by simply moving the brick.

2. Place the heat source and the pot of clean water directly under the rail.

3. Hang the fabric over the coat hanger and lower it into the hot water up to the point where you would like to begin bleeding the colour on.

4. Pour one litre of hot water into each of the two containers.

5. Stir the dye and salt into the one container. Stir in all three bags of dye first and when all the lumps are dissolved, stir in all three bags of salt.

6. Stir all of the soda ash (fixative) into the second container.

7. Add a scoop of the dye mixture to the pot using a measuring cup and stir constantly throughout the process.

8. Add a scoop of soda ash in the same way.

9. Raise the fabric a little out of the liquid.

10. Keep stirring for five minutes.

11. In case you should splash dye in an unwanted place, blast it immediately with a stream of clean cold water from a spray bottle to remove what you can before continuing.

12. Dose in more colour and soda ash.

13. Raise the fabric.

14. Repeat the process until you have a dark bleed along the bottom of the cloth. If you want a more drastic colour change than you are getting because your scarf is shorter than mine, you can add more dye each time to increase the rate of change. Be careful, though, as this might also cause a straight line to appear across the work.

15. Continue until the fabric rises completely out of the pot.

16. Wash the fabric well in clean water until the water runs clear and no more colour comes out. I recommend that you hold it under a running tap with the lightest colour at the top for best results. This way you do not wash the excess brown dye over the delicate creamy background and run the risk of staining it.

17. Add a small dash of fabric softener to the last rinse for softness.

18. Dry carefully, hanging over a coat hanger in exactly the way that you hung it to make it. If you hang it any other way, you run the risk of getting dark brown dye on the creamy white bits.

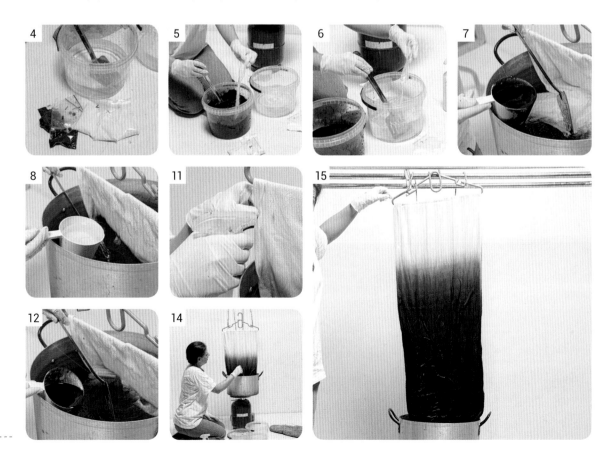

Pastel dip-dye

YOU WILL NEED

Patience

Heavyweight habotai silk scarf

Turquoise Slipstream Dye

Two containers for mixing chemicals

Gas bottle or stove

Large pot

Stirring implements

Measuring cup

Spray bottle

Coat hanger

Clothing rail or pole

Ski rope

A brick with holes in

In the previous project we looked at adding the finish to an existing colour. We put the brown over the cream and the cream was still visible on the finished work. What do you do if you want the bleed to cover the cloth, with none of the original background cloth showing?

To achieve this look, you have to layer a base coat of colour over the white cloth before you put the fabric on the coat hanger to apply the graded colour.

1. Start by building a structure that you can hang your fabric from. I used a clothing rail for this project. You might find that a washing line or a pole between two walls might work as well for you, depending on the size of your project and the heat source you decide to use. I hang the fabric over a coat hanger and then suspend that from ropes going over the top of the clothing rail. The brick is attached to the end of the ropes as a counterweight so that the fabric does not slip into the pot of dye completely. This contraption allows me to slowly raise and lower the fabric into the dye as I need to by simply moving the brick.

2. Place the heat source and the pot of clean water directly under the rail.

3. Pour one litre of hot water into each of the two mixing containers.

4. Stir the turquoise dye and salt into the one container and when all the lumps are dissolved, stir in the salt.

5. Stir the soda ash (fixative) into the second container.

6. Add a scoop of the dye mixture to the pot using a measuring cup and stir well.

7. Add a scoop of soda ash in the same way.

8. Stir the fabric into this mixture for 10 minutes.

9. Remove the fabric from the dye and hang it over the coat hanger, dangling into the dye from the point where you would like the colour to begin darkening.

Tie-dyed scarves

117

10. Dose in some more colour and fixative and stir continuously throughout.

11. Raise the fabric a little bit out of the liquid.

12. Keep stirring for five minutes.

13. Dose in more colour.

14. Raise the fabric.

15. Repeat the process until you have a gentle bleed of colour along the cloth. If you want a more drastic colour change than you are getting because your scarf is shorter than mine, you can add more dye each time to increase the rate of change. Be careful, though, as this might also cause a straight line to appear across the work.

16. Continue until the fabric rises completely out of the pot.

17. Wash the fabric well in clean water until the water runs clear and no more colour comes out. I recommend that you hold it under a running tap with the lightest colour at the top for best results.

18. Add a small dash of fabric softener to the last rinse for softness.

Dip-dye cheat

Lightweight habotai silk scarf

Overlocking thread or string

Golden Yellow, Pink and Turquoise Slipstream Dye

Container for mixing dye

Large bucket

Kettle and hot water

Stirring implement

Crocodile clamp

There is a very easy way to get a similar result and I prefer to use this technique when I need to make a dip-dyed look quickly, without all the fuss of building the jig. Very few people actually notice the difference between the one technique and the other so I will show you both and you can decide which one best suits your needs.

Stick to the controlled methodology for a smooth finish, while you can use this methodology when the outcome can be magical and slightly textured.

1. Work with dry fabric. This silk sticks to itself when wet.
2. Fold the fabric in half and in half again over your hand.
3. Gently bind the folds in place with a loose swirl of overlocking thread or string.
4. Fill the container with very hot water from the kettle and mix in the golden yellow dye, the salt and the soda ash in the usual way. Stir until all of the lumps are dissolved.
5. Place the scarf in the dye one third of the way up the fabric. Expect the colour to bleed further. Do not overthink it. Clamp the scarf to the side of the bigger bucket using a crocodile clamp and leave it to stand for an hour.
6. Remove the scarf from the yellow dye. Squeeze out the excess dye.

7. Fill the container with very hot water from the kettle and mix in the pink dye, the salt and the soda ash in the usual way. Stir until all of the lumps are dissolved.

8. Place the scarf in the dye one third of the way up the fabric from the other side. Expect the colour to bleed further. Do not overthink it. Clamp the scarf to the side of the bigger bucket so that it hangs into the liquid from above.

9. Leave it to stand for an hour.

10. Remove the fabric from the dye and squeeze out the excess. Mix the turquoise dye in the usual way, turn the fabric so that you are holding the ends and the middle of the scarf is hanging into the dye from above. Secure the fabric in this position with a crocodile clamp and leave it to stand for an hour.

11. Remove the fabric from the dye and squeeze out the excess dye. Wash this lightweight scarf out under clean running water.

12. Add a small dash of fabric softener to the last rinse for softness.

8

8

10

10

Tie-dyed scarves

Diagonal striping

You can turn the striped effect onto the diagonal on the cloth by changing one small thing in the way you bind the cloth at the start. I used a lightweight habotai silk for this project.

YOU WILL NEED

Lightweight habotai silk scarf

Overlocking thread or string

Red and Purple Slipstream Dye

Container for mixing dye

Kettle and hot water

Stirring implement

Crocodile clamp

1. Work with dry fabric. This thin habotai silk sticks to itself when wet.
2. Grip the fabric from one corner. Pull the fabric tight from that point and then wrap the strip lightly around the palm of your hand.
3. Lightly bind the folds in place using overlocking thread or string.
4. Half-fill the container with very hot water from the kettle and mix in the red slipstream dye, the salt and the soda ash in the usual way. Stir until all of the lumps are dissolved.
5. Place the scarf in the red dye halfway up the fabric. Expect the colour to bleed further. Do not overthink it. Clamp the scarf to the side of the container using a crocodile clamp and leave it to stand for an hour.
6. Remove the scarf from the red dye. Squeeze out the excess dye.
7. Half-fill the container with very hot water from the kettle and mix in the purple dye, the salt and the soda ash in the usual way. Stir until all of the lumps are dissolved.
8. Turn the scarf over and place the undyed section into the purple dye, halfway up the bundle. Expect the colour to bleed further. Do not overthink it. Clamp the scarf to the side of the container so that it hangs into the liquid from above.
9. Leave it to stand for an hour.
10. Remove the fabric from the dye and squeeze out the excess dye. Wash this lightweight scarf out under clean running water.
11. Add a small dash of fabric softener to the last rinse for softness.

Softest textures

YOU WILL NEED

Lightweight habotai silk scarf
Overlocking thread or string
Brown Slipstream Dye
Two containers for mixing dye
Kettle and hot water
Stirring implement

If you are not into bright, garish colours and prefer soft gentle colour and texture, then this is the project for you. This pattern is very easy to do and it translates very well into any pastel shade. For pastel-coloured dye, you just add a lot more water to your strong mixtures. There is no need to change the chemical ratio, just add more water by eye to reach the shade that you like.

You can also use smaller quantities of chemical powders to achieve a lighter shade.

The chiffon silk that we used for this project is so light that we added some heavy shell beads in a matching colour along the edge so that it drapes nicely.

1. Work with dry fabric.
2. Place the fabric on the table and crush it into random creases with your fingertips.
3. Bind the folds in place with overlocking thread or string. Work around the bundle, pulling the folds tighter and tighter as you go until you have a very compact bundle of fabric.
4. Fill the first container with very hot water from the kettle and mix in the brown dye, the salt and the soda ash in the usual way. Stir until all of the lumps are dissolved.
5. Pour just-boiled water into the second container and add a splash of the strong mixture into it until you get the pastel shade that you want. The leftover colour can be used for another project.
6. Place the scarf in the dye, stir it around for a little while and then submerge it under the surface of the liquid. Leave it to stand for an hour.
7. Remove the fabric from the dye and squeeze out the excess dye. Wash this lightweight scarf out under clean running water.
8. Add a small dash of fabric softener to the last rinse for softness.

2
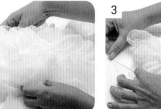

3

3

6

124

Hot pink crush

YOU WILL NEED

Raw silk scarf

Overlocking thread or string

Pink Slipstream Dye

Container for mixing dye

Kettle and hot water

Stirring implement

The same pattern in a strong colour is striking and bold without being too busy. This texture works very well for fabrics for quilting and fibre art projects. I used a raw silk with a crisp texture because it gives crisp, crackled marks with this binding technique.

1. Work with damp fabric as it is easier to bind.
2. Place the fabric on the table and crush the fabric into random creases with your fingertips.
3. Bind the folds in place with overlocking thread or string. Work around the bundle, pulling the folds tighter and tighter as you go until you have a very compact bundle of fabric.
4. Fill the container with very hot water from the kettle and mix in the pink dye, the salt and the soda ash in the usual way. Stir until all of the lumps are dissolved.
5. Place the scarf in the dye, stir it around for a little while and then submerge it under the surface of the liquid. Leave it to stand for an hour.
6. Remove the fabric from the dye and squeeze out the excess dye. Wash this lightweight scarf out under clean running water.
7. Add a small dash of fabric softener to the last rinse for softness.

Caribbean cool

This crushed pattern can be transformed quite radically by using three colours rather than one. For this project I worked on a textured Damask silk to add more depth to the finished work.

The pattern on the shiny silk lends itself well to bling embellishments. Glue or stitch on some shiny blue sequins and transform this silk into a glam accessory that you can wear out to any big evening event.

1. Work with damp fabric. Place the fabric on the table and crush it into random creases with your fingertips.
2. Bind the folds in place with overlocking thread or string. Work around the bundle, pulling the folds tighter and tighter as you go until you have a very compact bundle of fabric.
3. Mix a small quantity of hot turquoise dye and pour it into the bottom of the container. There must be just enough dye to come halfway up the edge of the fabric once it has been lowered into the container.
4. Place the fabric into this shallow bath of turquoise dye. Leave it to stand for an hour.
5. Remove it from the dye and gently squeeze out the excess dye.

6. Mix the hot lime green dye in the usual way and pour a very small quantity of the hot lime green dye in the bottom of the container. There must be just enough dye to come halfway up the edge of the fabric once it has been lowered into the container. Flip the bundle over and place the other side of the bundle in the lime green dye.

7. Leave it to stand for an hour.

8. Remove the fabric from the dye and gently squeeze out the excess.

9. Pour just-boiled water into the second container and mix strong hot navy blue dye into the water in the usual way.

10. Drop the whole scarf into the mixture and stir for five seconds. Then remove it completely from the dye and leave it to stand for an hour.

11. Wash this lightweight scarf out under clean running water.

12. Add a small dash of fabric softener to the last rinse for softness.

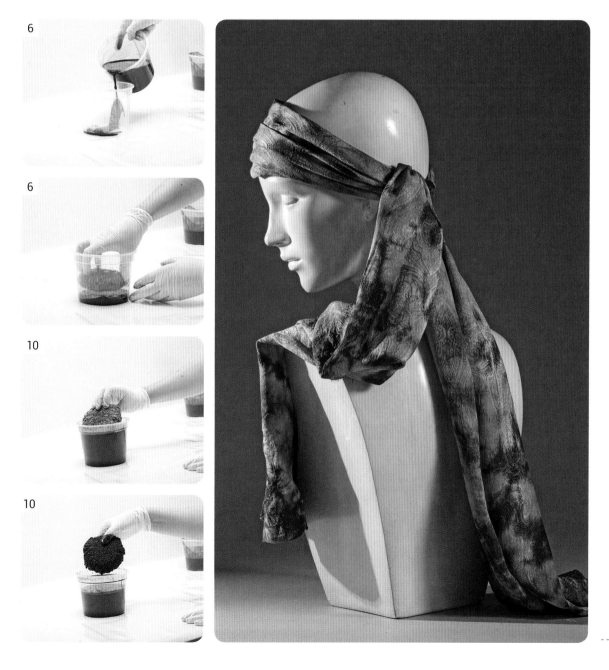

The zebra

YOU WILL NEED
Raw silk slub with a gritty texture
Fork
Three elastic bands
Black Slipstream Dye
Container for mixing dye
Kettle and hot water
Stirring implement

I have always felt that the zebra is a wonderful symbol of Africa and this pattern looks just like zebra striping. This scarf will match any plain black outfit and allow you to accessorise it in an ethnic way with large, chunky jewellery. I love the way this heavy raw silk slub drapes.

1. Work with damp fabric.
2. Take the fabric along the cut edge and fold it in half so that the two cut edges line up.
3. One third of the way down the edge of the cut edges, you attach the fork by sliding the cloth in-between the teeth of the fork.
4. Use the fork as a handle to grip the fabric as you turn it. I tell children to try to get all of the spaghetti onto their fork.
5. Keep turning the fabric and gently folding the creases around the centre until you end up with a shape a bit like a Chelsea bun.
6. Put three elastic bands around the bundle to hold the folds in place.
7. Add enough water from your just-boiled kettle to the container to cover the project. Mix in the black dye, the salt and the soda ash in the usual way. Stir until all of the lumps are dissolved.
8. Place the scarf in the dye, jiggle it around a little and make sure that it is submerged under the liquid.
9. Leave it to stand for an hour before rinsing thoroughly.
10. Add a splash of fabric softener to the final rinse for softness.

Classic two-stripe

`//////////////////////////////////////////////////////////////////////////////////` EASY

A simple striped border along the cloth is all that is needed to turn a plain coloured scarf into a special handmade piece that pops.

1. Fold the scarf in half and in half again. Fold it again and again in this same way until you have a strip of folded fabric layers about 10 cm wide.

2. Fold that back in half again so that the selvedge from both edges of the fabric is lined up.

3. Scrunch the fabric together along the selvedge and wrap an elastic band very tightly around the end of the fabric, about 2 cm from the edge.

4. Add a second elastic band about 2 cm down from the first one. They must be bound very tightly.

5. Pour just-boiled water from the kettle into your container. Stir in the purple dye, the salt and the soda ash in the usual way.

6. Stir in the fabric immediately while the mixture is still steaming hot.

7. Submerge it under the surface of the liquid and leave it to stand for an hour before rinsing.

8. Rinse the fabric thoroughly under clean running water until there is no more excess dye escaping from the fibre. Add a splash of fabric softener to the final rinse for extra softness.

9. Accessorise with a crochet embellishment.

Centre panel two-stripe

YOU WILL NEED

Lightweight habotai silk scarf

Elastic band

Red and Black Slipstream Dye

Container for mixing dye

Kettle and hot water

Stirring implement

Crocodile clamp

By making a couple of small changes to the methodology of the previous project, it is possible to create a centre panel on your scarf. This pattern will dress down as a top for daywear on the beach and it will dress up as an evening accessory.

1. Work with dry fabric.
2. Fold the fabric in half along the selvedge. Fold it in half again and again to create parallel fan folds until you end up with a bundle of folded fabric about 10 cm wide.
3. Fold the strip of fabric back in half again.
4. Bind the elastic band very tightly across the middle of the bundle.
5. Half-fill the container with very hot water from the kettle and mix in the red slipstream dye, the salt and the soda ash in the usual way. Stir until all of the lumps are dissolved.
6. Place the scarf in the red dye up to the elastic band, halfway up the fabric. Expect the colour to bleed further. Do not overthink it. Clamp the scarf to the side of the container using a crocodile clamp and leave it to stand for an hour.
7. Remove the scarf from the red dye. Squeeze out the excess dye.
8. Half-fill the container with very hot water from the kettle and mix in the black dye, the salt and the soda ash in the usual way. Stir until all of the lumps are dissolved.
9. Turn the scarf over and place the undyed section into the black dye, halfway up the bundle. Expect the colour to bleed further. Do not overthink it. Clamp the scarf to the side of the container so that it hangs into the liquid from above.
10. Leave it to stand for an hour.
11. Remove the fabric from the dye and squeeze out the excess. Wash this lightweight scarf out under clean running water.
12. Add a small dash of fabric softener to the last rinse for softness.

2

3

4

6

Diamonds are a girl's best friend

YOU WILL NEED

Crêpe-de-chine silk scarf

Overlocking thread or thin string

A few elastic bands

Container for mixing dye

Lime Green Slipstream Dye

Stirring implement

Although many people love spiral tie-dye, my favourite pattern to play with must be the diamond. I enjoy playing with placement and colour to find fresh new ways of interpreting this simple concept.

I made this pattern on a large piece of crêpe de Chine so that I could play with the placement of the shapes and so that I would have the option to wear it as a sarong on the beach.

1. Fold the scarf in half and in half again.
2. Turn it in the other direction and fold it in half along the other dimension.
3. Fold back one corner of the rectangular shape at 45 degrees.
4. Using that fold as a guide, create parallel fan folds about 5 cm apart.
5. Once the whole piece of fabric is folded up into these concertina folds, you can bind them in place using overlocking thread or string.
6. The pressure created by the string will not be enough to clearly define the outline of the diamond so you will need to wrap elastic bands, very tightly around the cloth over the string to tighten everything up before it goes into the dye. It is very tricky to get the elastics on tightly enough if you do not first secure everything with string because the folds spring open in the wrestling. Place the elastic bands at regular intervals along the bundle.
7. Pour just-boiled water from the kettle into your container. Stir in the lime green dye, the salt and the soda ash in the usual way.
8. Stir in the fabric immediately while the mixture is still steaming hot. Give it a good jiggle so that the colour penetrates the many layers of folded cloth.
9. Submerge it under the surface of the liquid and leave it to stand for an hour before rinsing.
10. Wash the fabric thoroughly in clean water. Once most of the excess colour has been removed, you can remove the bindings.
11. Add a splash of fabric softener to the final rinse for extra softness.
12. Dry indoors over a coat hanger.

1

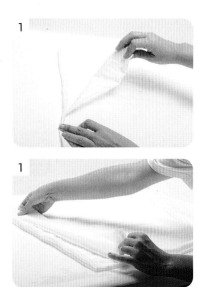

1

2

3

4

5

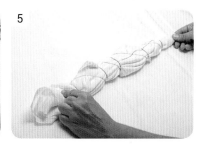

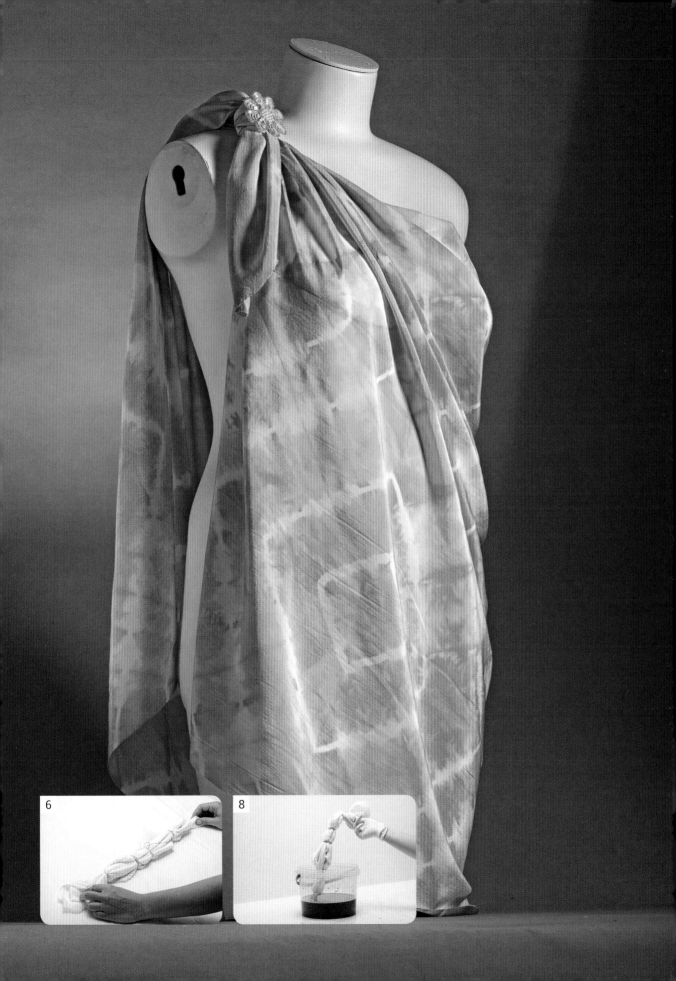

Corporate diamonds

YOU WILL NEED

Lightweight habotai silk scarf

Four elastic bands

Container for mixing dye

Red and Black Slipstream Dye

Stirring implement

Crocodile clamp

Red and black are classic corporate colours and the orderly geometric design is well-suited to office wear. This is one of my favourite scarves to make during demonstrations and no matter what colours I play it out in, it is always a hit with my students.

1. Fold the scarf in half and in half again along the selvedge of the fabric. Keep doing this until you end up with a strip of folded fabric about 12 cm wide.
2. Turn it in the other direction and fold it in half along the other dimension.
3. Fold the ends under to make a square shape.
4. Fold back one corner of the square at 45 degrees to create a triangle.
5. Bind an elastic band very tightly across the point and base of your triangle.
6. Add another elastic band on either side.
7. Pour just-boiled water from the kettle into your container. Stir in the red dye, the salt and the soda ash in the usual way.

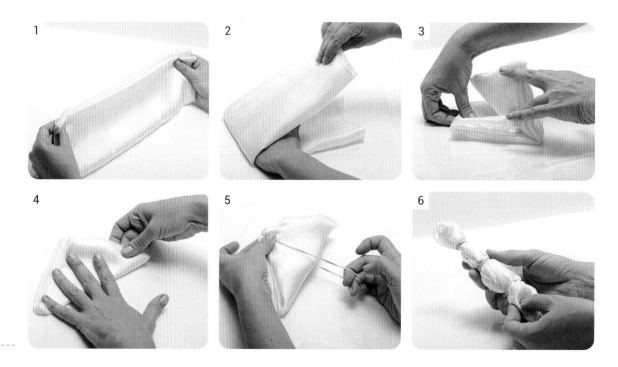

8. Stir in the fabric immediately while the mixture is still steaming hot up to the elastic band in the middle. Give it a good jiggle so that the colour penetrates the many layers of folded cloth.

9. Submerge it under the surface of the liquid up to that mark, clamp it to the side of the container using a crocodile clamp to keep it in place and leave it to stand for an hour.

10. Remove it from the dye and squeeze out the excess dye.

11. Pour just-boiled water from the kettle into your container. Stir in the black dye, the salt and the soda ash in the usual way.

12. Turn the bundle the other way and jiggle the undyed section of the scarf in the black dye to get the colour through all of the layers of cloth. Clamp the fabric to the side of the container in the correct position and leave it to stand for an hour.

13. Remove the fabric from the dye and squeeze out the excess dye. Wash the fabric thoroughly in clean water. Once most of the excess colour has been removed, you can remove the bindings.

14. Add a splash of fabric softener to the final rinse for extra softness.

15. Dry indoors over a coat hanger.

8

9

12

12

Native American motif

YOU WILL NEED

Coarse silk slub with a gritty texture

Overlocking thread or thin string

Container for mixing dye

Turquoise, Navy, Purple and Black Slipstream Dye

Stirring implement

Large bucket

Crocodile clamp

This diamond project on the coarse silk slub has a definite Native American look and feel. I have also played it out in red, orange, blue and black on chiffon silk for a Ndebele feel for the South African fashion industry.

Try this pattern on different fabrics and see how many different looks you can create by manipulating fabric source and colour choice. I have found it to be fail-safe when I want to create drama in a piece.

1. Fold the scarf in half and in half again in the other direction.
2. Fold back one corner of the square at 45 degrees to create a fold coming from the centre point of the scarf.
3. Use this fold as a guideline to create parallel concertina folds in the fabric.
4. Use the overlocking thread to bind the folds securely in place. Pinch it at regular intervals by going around and around with the thread in the same place about five to ten times, depending on the strength of your string and the structure of the fabric. Pinch the fabric in six places along the length of the cloth in this way.
5. Pour just-boiled water from the kettle into your container. Stir in the turquoise dye, the salt and the soda ash in the usual way.
6. Stir in the fabric immediately while the mixture is still steaming hot up to the last segment of the bundle. Give it a good jiggle so that the colour penetrates the many layers of folded cloth.
7. Submerge it under the surface of the liquid up to just before the last segment, clamp it to the side of the container using a crocodile clamp to keep it in place and leave it to stand for an hour.

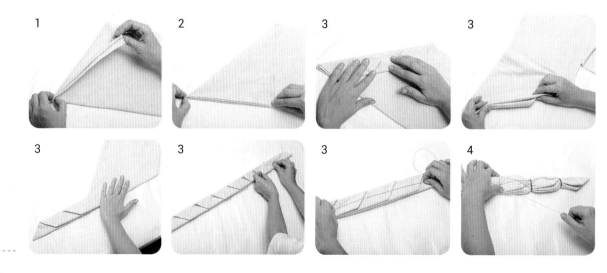

8. Remove it from the dye and squeeze out the excess moisture.

9. Pour just-boiled water from the kettle into your container. Stir in the navy dye, the salt and the soda ash in the usual way.

10. Return the bundle to the navy dye in the same way that you did for the first colour, except that you will move the dye level down a segment.

11. Clamp the fabric to the side of the bucket to hold it in place and leave it to stand for an hour.

12. Remove the fabric from the dye and squeeze out the excess dye.

13. Pour just-boiled water from the kettle into your container. Stir in the purple dye, the salt and the soda ash in the usual way.

14. Stir in the fabric immediately while the mixture is still steaming hot up to the end of the first segment of the bundle. Give it a good jiggle so that the colour penetrates the many layers of folded cloth.

15. Clamp it to the side of the container using a crocodile clamp to keep it in place and leave it to stand for an hour.

16. Remove it from the dye and squeeze out the excess dye.

17. Pour just-boiled water from the kettle into your container. Stir in the black dye, the salt and the soda ash in the usual way.

18. Turn the bundle over and work from the other side. Hang the scarf from above into the black dye to cover the final segment.

19. Clamp the fabric to the side of the bucket to hold it in place and leave it to stand for an hour.

20. Remove the fabric from the dye and squeeze out the excess dye.

21. Wash the fabric thoroughly in clean water. Once most of the excess colour has been removed, you can remove the bindings.

22. Add a splash of fabric softener to the final rinse for extra softness.

23. Dry indoors over a coat hanger.

6

7

10

11

14

15

18

19

Acknowledgements

A book is a team effort and by the end of one there is always a long list of people to thank. These are the important people who played a pivotal role in me getting this project finished in time. Thank you to:
Clara Jansen for helping me make the more than 200 step-by-step samples for the shoot and for writing the forward for this book. This Textile Design student from TUT is committed and talented and she has become an invaluable part of my team.

The **Metz Press team**, especially **Wilsia Metz** for having faith in me, **Lindie Metz** for her fantastic production support, **Claudine Henchie** for the great look and feel of the book, and **Ivan Naude** for absolutely getting what I do and knowing how to best portray it in pictures.

Justine Leroy for getting me to my shoots when my car was not running and for help with the preparation and styling of fabrics during shooting. Also for the background information about Penny Leroy, her grandmother. Linda Scrace and Chemosol for supplying the ink that we used to print the samples. **Anthony Brummer** for allowing me to use his car to get to shoots.

To my friends and family who supported me patiently through the process. To **Mom** for feeding me when I was too busy think about food. To **Vivienne** and **Eugene** for dragging me off to boat parties when all the pressure got too much and I needed a break.

And finally to my customers, your joy inspires me to always keep doing what I do and I hope that you enjoy reading and using it as much as I did making it.

Melanie Brummer
April 2013

www.facebook.com/dyeandprints
www.dyeandprints.co.za

Published by Stackpole Books
5067 Ritter Road
Mechanicsburg, PA 17055
www.stackpolebooks.com

First published in 2013 by Metz Press
www.metzpress.co.za

Copyright © Metz Press 2015
Text copyright © Melanie Brummer
Photographs copyright © Metz Press

Publisher	Wilsia Metz
Photographer	Ivan Naudé
Design	Claudine Henchie
Editor	Nikki Metz
Proofreader	Francie Botes
Reproduction	Color/Fuzion, Green Point
Print production	Andrew de Kock
Printed and bound by	TWP Sdn. Bhd., Malaysia
ISBN	978-0-8117-1473-0